THE GOSPEL

ACCORDING TO *Matthew*

JENNIFER WALKER

LUCIDBOOKS

I would like to dedicate this workbook to my mom, dad, and husband.
Their love for God, His Word and His people are truly supernatural.

How the Questions Are Designed (Inductive Method)

Examination (E) – What does the text say?

Interpretation (I) – What does the text mean?

Transformation (T) – How does the text change me?

This study uses the English Standard Version (ESV) of the Bible unless otherwise specified.

CONTENTS

MATTHEW 1

God Became a Man to Give Sinners a New Life

AIM: God became a man to give sinners a new life.

Scripture to Memorize:

She will bear a son, and you shall call his name Jesus, for he will save his people from their sins.

—Matt. 1:21

Attribute of God: Savior

God rescues and saves sinners. We are all sinners and deserve death and to spend eternity in hell. We are not able to save ourselves, so God sent His perfect Son to rescue us from the enslavement of sin. Jesus lived the perfect, obedient life that we cannot, and He satisfied God's wrath by taking the punishment of death in our place on the cross. All who place their faith in Jesus have been freed from sin—from its penalty, power, and presence. This is a past, present, and future reality. The moment a person places their faith in Jesus Christ, they are free from sin's guilt and punishment. The Holy Spirit empowers the believers to turn from sin and obey and follow Jesus throughout their life. One day, the believer will be reunited with Jesus and see Him face-to-face and be free from the presence of sin for all eternity.

Doctrine: God the Son

God, the Son, is Jesus Christ. He was a prophet, a teacher, and a man. However, the Bible tells us He is considerably much more. The Son is the Second Person in the Holy Trintiy and existed with the Father and the Spirit from eternity past. There has never been a time when the Son did not exist. He participated in the creation of the world. The Gospels tell us how He humbled Himself by taking on a fleshly, bodily form, born to a virgin, in order to save humanity from their sins. Even though He was a man, Jesus did not stop being divine. He was both fully man and fully God. He led a perfect and obedient life fulfilling all biblical prophecy, and at the right time He died on behalf of sinners. He rose on the third day defeating death and proving His authority over all things including power over sin. Jesus ascended into Heaven and is seated at the right hand of the Father, interceding on our behalf. He will one day return to earth to judge the world and set up His eternal kingdom where His people will dwell with Him forever.

The truth that God came near to us is the greatest truth of all time. The one who created the trees sat under them and taught His disciples. He designed the very desert the devil would tempt Him in. He came to reveal God to us, not just as a sign or a partial revelation, but as the full revelation of God, Himself. He is the radiance and glory of God and the exact imprint of His nature. (Hebrews 1:3) His Word upholds and sustains the entire universe. He left the glory and splendor of Heaven so that we could draw near to Him, and it is only through Jesus that we are able to draw near to a Holy God. He has opened the way for fellowship with God the Father. There is no other way to God except by grace alone, through faith alone, in Jesus Christ alone.

Day 1: Introduction

1. Who wrote the Gospel of Matthew? Write what you know about him.

_____

_____

_____

2. When was it written?

_____

_____

_____

3. To whom was it written?

_____

_____

_____

4. In what style was it written?

_____

_____

_____

_____

5. What are the central themes of the book?

_____

_____

_____

_____

Day 2: Read Matthew 1

1. In two to three sentences, summarize what happens in this chapter.

   Chapter 1

_____

_____

_____

_____

2. What are your thoughts on reading through the genealogies found in Scripture? Why do you think this?

_____

_____

_____

_____

Day 3: Read Matthew 1:1-17

1. (E,I) Matthew starts his book with an extensive genealogy. Fill in the blanks from verse 1. Who is at the center of the genealogy?

    "The book of the genealogy of _____, the son of _____, the son of _____."

2. (I) Why might Matthew have begun his book with the genealogy of Jesus? What was the importance of including names such as Abraham, Jacob, and David? (See Genesis 12:1-3, 22:18, 35:10-12, and 2 Samuel 7:8, 12-13 to help with your answer.)

    _____

    _____

    _____

3. (E,I) Women were not usually included in genealogies, yet Matthew includes five. Give the background of each woman Matthew mentions in Jesus's genealogy.

    Tamar – Genesis 38

    _____

    _____

    _____

    Rahab – Joshua 2, 6:17-25

    _____

    _____

    _____

    Ruth – Ruth 1, 4:13-17

    _____

    _____

    _____

"Wife of Uriah" – 2 Samuel 11:1-5, 12:24

_____

_____

_____

Mary – Luke 1:26-56

_____

_____

_____

4. (I) Why do you think Matthew included these women in Jesus's genealogy?

    _____

    _____

    _____

5. (E) What pattern/repeated phrase do you see in Matthew's organization of names in the genealogy?

    _____

    _____

    _____

6. (E) How does Matthew deviate from the repeated phrase in verse 16? With which descendant?

    _____

    _____

    _____

    _____

7. (I) What do you think Matthew wants us to understand in doing this?

_____

_____

_____

_____

8. (I,T) Genesis 3:15 is often called the protoevangelium, or first Gospel, because it is the Bible's first prediction of a Savior brought forth through "the woman's seed." How do you see God's faithfulness in verses 1-17? How have you seen God's faithfulness in your own life?

_____

_____

_____

Day 4: Read Matthew 1:18-23

1. (E,I) Fill in the blanks from verse 18. What is the significance of this statement?

    "Now the birth of Jesus took place in this way. When his mother Mary had been betrothed to Joseph, _____ she was found to be with child _____."

2. (E) Fill in the blanks.

    Who was Jesus's mother (v. 18)? _____

    Who was Jesus's father (vv. 18, 20)? _____

    Who was Jesus's adoptive father (vv. 19-25)? _____

3. (I) Explain why the virgin birth is important to orthodox Christianity. Use Scripture to give evidence of your answer.

    _____

    _____

    _____

4. (E,) Joseph is not aware of what really happened until verse 20. Read Deuteronomy 22:23-24. What would have been lawful for Joseph to do at this point? How did Joseph instead respond to Mary's pregnancy?

    _____

    _____

    _____

    _____

5. (I) What does this reveal about his character? How does this already point us forward to Jesus? (Matthew 9:13, 12:7)

    _____

    _____

    _____

    _____

6. (T) What can modern-day Christians learn from Joseph's response to a desperate circumstance?

    _____

    _____

    _____

    _____

7. (E,I) Give the two names and their meanings that God gives to Mary and Joseph's son (vv. 21, 23).

    _____

    _____

    _____

8. (T) What does the nature of both names mean to you personally?

_____

_____

_____

_____

9. (I) Read Isaiah 7:14. How does this prophecy find fulfillment in Jesus Christ?

_____

_____

_____

_____

10. (I) What does this reveal about God?

_____

_____

_____

_____

11. (T) In verses 20-23, God reassures and comforts Joseph with His Word. Describe a time the Lord reassured and comforted you through His Word.

_____

_____

_____

_____

_____

Day 5: Matthew 1:24-25

1. (E,I) How did Joseph demonstrate his faith in verse 24? How does this fit with what we already know of his character?

    _____

    _____

    _____

2. (I) Describe how Joseph and Mary's obedience would have been costly.

    _____

    _____

    _____

3. (T) How has obeying God been costly for you?

    _____

    _____

    _____

    _____

Day 6: Commit what you learned to prayer. Reread Matthew 1.

Adoration:

Lord, I praise you for being my King and Savior. You are the promised hope of the world. I praise You for being the ultimate fulfillment from eternity past. You, Jesus, are the mercy of God in salvation.

Confession:

Father, forgive me when I focus on the mundane events in life with little or no thought of You. Forgive me when I am not obedient to You in my thoughts, words, and actions. Forgive me when I am unfaithful to You.

Thanksgiving:

Thank you, Father, for sending your Son who has the power and authority to forgive sin. Thank you for being faithful to Your Word. Thank you for Your steadfast love and care to even the smallest details in my life. Thank you for even setting Your gaze and favor upon me.

Supplication:

Global: I pray you use Your global Church to share the message of Your Gospel to reach every tribe, tongue, people group, and nation.

Local: Father, may our local church be a welcoming place of refuge for those who feel unworthy and broken. Help them know they do not walk alone. Give us opportunities to love others as You have loved us.

Personal: Father, help me be obedient to Your Word. Build my faith so I can follow after You and You alone.

MATTHEW 2-4

Jesus Is the Better Adam, Better David, and Better Israel

AIM: Jesus is the better Adam, better David, and better Israel.

Scripture to Memorize:

From that time Jesus began to preach, saying, "Repent, for the kingdom of heaven is at hand."

–Matt. 4:17

Attribute of God: Omnipotent

God has power over all things in all ways. He will accomplish all His plans and purposes. Nothing is able to stop him. He is source of all life, and his power sustains the whole world. Without him everything would crumble. All of life would perish were it not for God's preservation in His creation. Even the devil, death, and sin are limited. God has defeated them all. He can do everything that is in accord with His character. Jesus in His incarnation was omnipotent. He had power over sickness, nature, sin, Satan, and even death. God has the power to keep all His promises.

Doctrine: Kingdom of God

The Kingdom of God is the invisible, spiritual realm that resides and rules in the hearts of all those who believe in Jesus for salvation. It is sometimes referred to as the "Kingdom of Heaven" and appears over 60 times in the Gospels. The Kingdom is God's rule over all creation from eternity past to the present and will one day be a visible, physical kingdom established on Earth where everyone will proclaim Jesus as King and His reign will be forever and ever. The present visible kingdom is demonstrated in the life of God's people. John Calvin says this is the task of the Church; to make the invisible kingdom visible. Believers are citizens of the kingdom of God and are to reflect His very character. We are to bear witness to the kingship of Jesus in every aspect of our lives.

How can one enter into the kingdom of God? Simply put, by faith. This is why the Gospel must be preached. When the people respond to the message in faith, they are submitting to the rule and reign of God and they start to be transformed and renewed inwardly. Continued obedience and submission to the kingship and lordship of Christ will continue to grow within the person as they become more and more like Christ. Collectively the kingdom started small but continues to grow over time before engulfing the entire world. The Church is the historical proof of God's kingdom expansion.

God's kingdom is not like the kingdoms of this world, concerned with status and position, but characterized by character, heart, and serving others. Jesus says humility is the greatest in the kingdom. It allocates for dependency, self-denial, able to be taught, and helplessness. The world tells us these virtues are undesirable, but Jesus teaches these virtues promote honest faith in God and is rewarded by Him. It is His presence, His Kingdom, that is our great reward. How have you experienced this very blessing of the Kingdom in your own life?

Day 1: Read Matthew 2-4

1. In two to three sentences, summarize what happens in these chapters.

    Chapter 2

    _____

    _____

    _____

    Chapter 3

    _____

    _____

    _____

    Chapter 4

    _____

    _____

    _____

2. How many prophecies are fulfilled in just these chapters? Note them below.

    _____

    _____

    _____

Day 2: Read Matthew 2

Verses 1-6

1. (E,I) Bethlehem was a city in Judah that produced Davidic kings (Ruth, 1 Samuel 17). Read Micah 5:2. How is this prophecy fulfilled in Christ?

    _____

    _____

    _____

2. (E) Fill in the blanks from verse 2.

    "Where is he who has been born _____? For we saw his star when it rose and have come to _____."

3. (I) Were the wise men speaking about Herod, the King of the Jews, or someone else? How do you know?

    _____

    _____

    _____

4. (E,I) How were the Magi guided to Jesus? What does this reveal about God?

    _____

    _____

    _____

5. (T) How has God guided you to seek and know Him?

_____

_____

_____

6. (E,I) Who did Herod gather in verse 4? They quote Micah 5:2 in verses 5-6. How does this Old Testament prophecy concern Jesus?

_____

_____

_____

7. (E) Fill in the blanks with either Wise Men/Gentiles or Chief Priests and Scribes/Jews.

_____? were looking for the Messiah.

_____? were not looking for the Messiah.

8. (T) How does the above question reveal the people of God even today?

_____

_____

_____

Verses 7-12

9. (E,I) How is Jesus referred to in these verses? What do you think Matthew wants to communicate?

_____

_____

_____

_____

10. (E) How did the wise men respond upon seeing the Christ child (v. 11)? (Read Deuteronomy 6:13 and Matthew 4:10 for a better understanding of the significance of the wise men's actions.)

_____

_____

_____

_____

11. (I) Compare verse 11 with Psalm 72:10. How does this prophecy find a specific fulfillment in the wise men?

_____

_____

_____

_____

12. (E) Compare verse 11 with Isaiah 66:18-19. How does this prophecy find a general fulfillment in the wise men?

_____

_____

_____

_____

13. (T) Read verses 1-12 again and list all the ways the wise men were truly wise. What can we learn from them today?

_____

_____

_____

_____

14. (I) After rereading verses 1-12, compare and contrast our modern-day traditions of the wise men with the biblical text.

_____

_____

_____

Verses 13-15

15. (E,I) Compare verse 13 with verse 8. What was Herod's true intent concerning the Christ child? What heart motivation(s) was behind Herod's plan?

_____

_____

_____

_____

16. (T) Contrast the wise men's actions from verse 11 with Herod's actions mentioned in verse 13. How are these two responses still true today?

_____

_____

_____

_____

17. (E,I) Read Hosea 11:1. Who is the son referenced in that verse? Who is the Son referenced in verse 15? How is this prophecy fulfilled in Christ?

_____

_____

_____

_____

Verses 16-18

18. (E) How did Herod respond to Jesus's birth in verse 16?

_____

_____

_____

19. (I) What account in Exodus has a similar story (Exodus 1:15-22)?

_____

_____

_____

_____

20. (I) Read Jeremiah 31:15. This verse is referencing the grief and mourning of Israel as they were taken into captivity and the murder of the children during the invasion of Judea. How would the events described in these verses in Matthew be a general fulfillment of this prophecy?

_____

_____

_____

_____

21. (T) An evil ruler tried to thwart God's plans, but Jesus was born in spite of his plans. What does that teach us about God, His plans, and His purposes?

_____

_____

_____

_____

Verses 19-23

22. (E) Summarize how Joseph, Mary, and Jesus ended up in Nazareth.

_____

_____

_____

_____

23. There are two main ways to look at the meaning of verse 23.

One is by reading Isaiah 53:3 since some scholars agree that a Nazarene is a synonym for someone who is despised or detestable. (Nazareth is not mentioned in the Old Testament.) Note how this option has been fulfilled in Christ.

_____

_____

_____

Another is by reading Isaiah 11:1 since some scholars believe Nazareth is derived from the Hebrew word _netzer_, which means "sprout" or "branch." Note how this option has been fulfilled in Christ.

_____

_____

_____

24. (I) A contrast of two kingdoms is established for us in this chapter—an earthly kingdom ruled by mankind and a heavenly kingdom ruled by God. How would you characterize each kingdom so far?

_____

_____

_____

_____

25. (T) What two things can you practically do to demonstrate your love and devotion to Christ and His Kingdom?

_____

_____

_____

Day 3: Read Matthew 3

Verses 1-6

1. (E) Who was preaching in verse 1? What was his message (v. 2)?

    _____

    _____

    _____

2. (E) Look up the word *repent* in the dictionary and write a definition that best fits the way it is used in verse 2.

    _____

    _____

    _____

3. (I) Why is repentance an essential element to the Gospel message?

    _____

    _____

    _____

4. (T) What does it look like when a person truly repents?

    _____

    _____

5. (T) Is there something in your life you need to turn away from and turn toward? If so, prayerfully give it to God today.

_____

_____

_____

6. (I) In verse 3, Matthew quotes Isaiah 40:3. Read Isaiah 40:1–5. What do these verses tell you about the purpose of John's ministry?

_____

_____

_____

_____

7. (E) Describe John the Baptist from verse 4.

_____

_____

_____

_____

8. (E) Who else is described in a similar fashion as verse 4 (2 Kings 1:8)?

_____

_____

_____

_____

9. (E) Fill in the blanks.

    "And they were baptized by him in the river Jordan, _____."

10. (T) God uses events and circumstances to prepare His people for ministry. How have you seen this in your own life?

_____

_____

_____

Verses 7-12

11. (E,I) Who else came to the baptism in verse 7? Do you think they came to be baptized "with water for repentance"? Why or why not?

_____

_____

_____

12. (I) John the Baptist challenges the Pharisees and Sadducees to "bear fruit in keeping with repentance." Read Isaiah 2:12 and James 4:6. Which fruit bears repentance? Which fruit is characteristic of the religious leaders?

_____

_____

_____

13. (E) What would "bearing the fruit of repentance" look like practically (v. 6)?

_____

_____

_____

14. (E) What does John the Baptist rebuke the Pharisees and Sadducees for in verse 9?

_____

_____

15. (E) Who are the "real" sons of Abraham (Galatians 3:9, 29)?

_____

_____

_____

16. (T) What would the assumption of the Pharisees and Sadducees from verse 9 sound like today? (Example: I'm saved because I grew up in the Bible Belt.)

_____

_____

_____

17. (I) Paraphrase verse 10.

_____

_____

_____

18. (E) What is the difference between John's baptism and Jesus's baptism (v. 11)?

_____

_____

_____

19. (I) In verse 11, fire is directed toward a believer. In verse 12, it is directed toward an unbeliever. Explain how fire is applicable for both (believers: Zechariah 13:9, Numbers 31:23; unbelievers: Mark 9:47–48).

_____

_____

_____

_____

Verses 13-15

20. (E) What is the reason John the Baptist deters Jesus from being baptized (vv. 11, 14)?

_____

_____

_____

21. (I) What is surprising about Jesus's wanting to be baptized by John the Baptist? (See 1 John 3:5 for help.)

_____

_____

_____

22. (E) Fill in the blanks.

"But Jesus answered him, 'Let it be so now, for thus it is fitting for us to _____

_____.' "

23. (I) Baptism does not save, but it is a way for a person to identify with another. Read 2 Corinthians 5:21 and Romans 6:4, and describe the spiritual significance of Jesus's baptism. How is it already pointing us to the cross?

_____

_____

_____

24. (I) Paraphrase Jesus's response in verse 15.

_____

_____

_____

_____

Verses 16-17

25. (I) Read Isaiah 11:1–2 and 42:1. How do these prophecies find fulfillment in Jesus?

_____

_____

_____

26. (I) Match the miraculous event that occurred when Jesus was baptized with the best description of its significance.

Heavens opened up   Sign of God's affirmation and favor

Spirit of God descended and rested upon Him   Access to a holy God through Jesus

God expressed His pleasure in His Son   God's anointing and empowerment

_____

_____

_____

27. (T) Why are these truths important today for believers as adopted sons and daughters of God? Which of these truths is especially meaningful to you?

_____

_____

_____

Day 4: Read Matthew 4:1-11

Verses 1-11

1. (E) Who led Jesus into the wilderness? Why did He go there?

_____

_____

_____

_____

2. (E) Who never does the tempting (James 1:13)?

    _____

    _____

    _____

    _____

3. (E) Many great men in the Bible were proven in the wilderness. How many can you name?

    _____

    _____

    _____

    _____

4. (E) Read the following verses and note what each one teaches us about the devil/Satan.

    Isaiah 14:12-14

    _____

    John 8:44

    _____

    John 10:10

    _____

    Ephesians 2:1-3

    _____

    Revelation 20:3

    _____

    Revelation 20:10

    _____

5. (E) Read 1 John 2:16 and list the three avenues Satan uses to motivate wrong desires.

_____

_____

_____

6. (E,I) Using the chart below, parallel the temptations of Jesus with those of Adam and Eve and the Israelites. Fill in the chart by reading each verse and paraphrasing your findings. Write one of the three avenues Satan used and write whether or not each person passed or failed Satan's appeals. Some are completed for you.

Adam and Eve	The Israelites	Jesus
Genesis 3:6 "So when the woman saw that the tree was **good for food**…"	Exodus 16	Matthew 4:3
Satan's avenue: desire of the flesh	Satan's avenue:	Satan's avenue:
Genesis 3:6 Pass or Fail: Failed	Exodus 16:28 Pass or Fail:	Matthew 4:4 Pass or Fail:
Genesis 3:6 "and that it was a **delight to the eyes**…"	Exodus 32:1–8	Matthew 4:8–9 Satan took Jesus to a very high mountain and showed Him all the kingdoms of the world. He told Jesus He could have all of them if He would worship him.
Satan's avenue:	Satan's avenue:	Satan's avenue: desire of the eyes
Genesis 3:6 Pass or Fail:	Exodus 20:3 Pass or Fail:	Matthew 4:10 Pass or Fail: Pass

Adam and Eve	The Israelites	Jesus
Genesis 3:6 "and that the tree was to **be desired to make one wise**."	Exodus 17:1-7 The Israelites grumbled against Moses and God about being thirsty. They did not trust God to provide. Moses asked why they would put God to the test. The Israelites' sin was unbelief.	Matthew 4:5-6
Satan's avenue:	Satan's avenue: Pride of life	Satan's avenue:
Genesis 3:6 Pass or Fail:	Exodus 17:7 Pass or Fail: Fail	Matthew 4:7 Pass or Fail:

7.   What are some reasons Jesus was led to be tempted (Matthew 3:15, Hebrews 2:14-18, 4:5, John 4:34, John 10:10)?

_____

_____

_____

8.   (I) How did Jesus counter Satan's attacks?

_____

_____

_____

9.   (T) How is this a model for us today in resisting temptation?

_____

_____

10. (E) Fill in the blanks from verses 10 and 11.

"Then, Jesus said to him, '_____

_____' (v. 10).

Then the _____ " (v. 11).

11. (I) What does this reveal about the authority of Jesus?

_____

_____

_____

12. (T) Read 1 Corinthians 10:13. How is this encouraging and challenging to you?

_____

_____

_____

13. (T) Describe a time the Holy Spirit led you through temptation to victory.

_____

_____

_____

Day 5: Read Matthew 4:12–25

Verses 12-17

1. (E) What do we learn about John the Baptist at the beginning of Jesus's ministry in verse 12?

_____

_____

_____

2. (E) What did Jesus do and where did He go when He heard about John's imprisonment?

    _____

    _____

    _____

    _____

3. (E) Fill in the blank from verse 15.

    "The land of Zebulun and the land of Naphtali, the way of the sea, beyond the Jordan, Galilee of the _____."

4. (I) Why do you think God allowed this circumstance to happen at this particular time? (Read Matthew 4:12-17, John 3:30, and Romans 1:16 to help with your answer.)

    _____

    _____

    _____

    _____

5. (T) What does this teach you about God and circumstances?

    _____

    _____

    _____

    _____

6. (I) Read Isaiah 9:1-2. How do verses 13-16 find fulfillment in Christ (John 8:12)?

    _____

    _____

    _____

    _____

7. (I) Compare 3:2 with 4:17. What do you notice?

_____

_____

_____

_____

Verses 18-25

8. (E) What are the names and occupations of the men Jesus calls in 4:18-20?

_____

_____

_____

_____

9. (E) What were the fishermen's responses to Jesus's call (vv. 20, 22)?

_____

_____

_____

10. (I) What does that teach us about the authority of Jesus?

_____

_____

_____

11. (T) What can you do to respond to God and His Word in such a way?

_____

_____

_____

12. (I) The men responded to Jesus's call immediately, leaving everything familiar behind. List what the men may have left behind to follow Jesus.

_____

_____

_____

_____

13. (T) What does it look like today for a true believer to "follow Christ"?

_____

_____

_____

_____

14. (E) What are the three main aspects of Christ's ministry found in verse 23?

_____

_____

_____

15. (I) What does verse 24 reveal about Christ?

_____

_____

_____

16. (E) How do the people respond to the ministry of Jesus in verses 24-25?

_____

_____

_____

Day 6: Commit what you learned to prayer. Reread Matthew 2-4.

Adoration:

"God, you are…."

Pray the attributes of God we studied this week back to God.

Confession:

"Lord, I confess…."

In light of the above and what we studied this week, what did you learn about yourself?

Thanksgiving:

"Thank you…."

What from this week's passage made your heart overflow with thanksgiving?

Supplication:

"I lift up…."

After reading this week's passage, what petitions do you need to ask of God?

Global: _____

Local: _____

Personal: _____

MATTHEW 5

A Godly Life Gives Testimony of the Saving Power of God

AIM: A godly life gives testimony to the saving power of God.

Scripture to Memorize:

Do not think that I have come to abolish the Law or the Prophets; I have not come to abolish them but to fulfill them.

—Matt. 5:17

Attribute of God: Righteous

God is always right and He is always good. God has no sin and is perfect in every way. God's laws are the plumbline to measure what is good and moral. They reveal His nature and character. God expects perfection from us, but even the best person cannot be righteous. Jesus was perfect in all His thoughts, attitudes, words, actions, and deeds. He obeyed every law perfectly, even the spirit of the law. Those who place their faith in Jesus, God sees as clothed with His Son's righteousness.

Doctrine: Righteousness

Righteousness is behavior that is morally justifiable or right. God is the only one who is perfectly righteous. When we are measured against God's standards of righteousness we all fall short because we have all sinned. There is not one human who is perfect in every thought, word, or deed. Jesus explained in his Sermon on the Mount, even when we falsely believe our external actions uphold acceptable behaviors, our hearts are still rebellious against God and do not honor or please him. The bad news is that we cannot attain perfect righteousness on our own. We cannot earn our favor with God or earn our way into Heaven. We cannot even understand ourselves correctly. We have all probably thought of ourselves at one time or another as a "good person." But, this is because we are measuring ourselves against the wrong standards. God's standards are the only ones that matter, and His standards mean we must be perfect.

The good news is righteousness is possible for humankind. The amazing truth is "God made him who knew no sin be sin for us, so that in him we might become the righteousness of God (2 Corinthians 5:21). Jesus lived a perfect, obedient life without ever sinning, and on the cross an exchange was made. He became sin for us, and His perfect righteousness was credited to us so that when we stand before a holy God, He will not see our sin, but the holy righteousness of His son, Jesus Christ. This is the only way to have access and fellowship with God, the Father. When we place our faith in Christ for our righteousness, our life changes. We no longer try to earn our salvation; instead, our deeds become the fruit of our salvation. God transforms us from the inside out and leads to a life that loves God and loves others.

Day 1: Read Matthew 5

1. In two to three sentences, summarize what happens in this chapter.

_____

_____

_____

2. How can Kingdom citizens reflect the character of God?

_____

_____

_____

Day 2: Read Matthew 5:1-12

Verses 1-2

1. (E) Where did Jesus go when He saw the crowds in verse 1?

_____

_____

_____

2. (E) When was the last time in Scripture that God delivered a message at the top of a mountain (Exodus 19)?

_____

_____

_____

3. (E) Name the groups that followed Jesus to the mountain.

_____

_____

_____

4. (I) Who was Jesus teaching to primarily? Who are "them" in verse 2?

_____

_____

_____

Verses 3-12

5. (I) Look up the word *blessed* and write a definition in your own words that best fits the way it is used in these verses.

_____

_____

_____

6. (E) List the eight Beatitudes and who Jesus considers blessed. (You do not need to write the reward.) One has been done for you.

a. _____

b. _____

c. Blessed are the meek.

d. _____

e. _____

f. _____

g. _____

h. _____

7. (T) Next, list a counterfeit (an opposite) condition the world would consider blessed that corresponds to each beatitude. One has been done for you.

a. _____

b. _____

c. Self-assertive and controlling

d. _____

e. _____

f. _____

g. _____

h. _____

8. (E,I) Finally, list the reward for all the Beatitudes and whether they have a past, present, or future fulfillment. (Some may have more than one answer.) One has been done for you. What does that tell us concerning the reality of the Kingdom?

a. _____

b. _____

c. For they shall inherit the earth – future fulfillment

d. _____

e. _____

f. _____

g. _____

h. _____

9. (T) How does having a correct view of God and a correct view of self contribute to the Beatitudes?

_____

_____

_____

10. (T) How have you personally experienced the blessing of one of the Beatitudes (pick one or two)?

_____

_____

_____

11. (T) How has God transformed you so that you desire what He considers blessed?

_____

_____

_____

12. (T) Which of the Beatitudes most convicted you? Ask God to develop it more in your life.

_____

_____

_____

Day 3: Read Matthew 5:13-16

Verses 13-16

1. (E) What is the purpose of salt?

_____

_____

THE GOSPEL ACCORDING TO MATTHEW

2. (I) How can Christians function as salt in this world?

    _____

    _____

    _____

3. (E) What is the purpose of light?

    _____

    _____

    _____

4. (T) Think back to Matthew 4:16 where Jesus is referred to as the Light. How can Christians be light (lower case *l*) in this world (Isaiah 42:6-7)?

    _____

    _____

    _____

5. (E) Summarize Jesus's main point in verses 13-16.

    _____

    _____

    _____

6. (T) How can God use you specifically to be salt and light to make a difference in the world?

    _____

    _____

    _____

Day 4: Read Matthew 5:17-20

Verses 17-20

1. Fill in the blanks from verse 17.

   "Do not think I have come to _____ the _____ or the _____; I have not come to _____ them but to _____ them."

2. (E) What are the Law and the Prophets Jesus is referring to (Luke 24:27, John 1:45)?

   _____

   _____

   _____

   _____

3. (I) What does Jesus want to communicate about the relationship between His ministry and the Old Testament? Why is that important? (Consider His audience.)

   _____

   _____

   _____

   _____

   _____

4. (I) How did Jesus fulfill the Law? The moral law (Hebrews 4:15)? The ceremonial laws and sacrifices (1 Peter 1:18-21)? The Old Testament prophecies (Luke 24:26-27)?

   _____

   _____

   _____

   _____

   _____

5. (I) Look at verse 19. Circle the main point Jesus wants to communicate about those who follow Him.

   They must keep all the Old Testament laws.

   They must handle God's Word carefully.

6. (I) Jesus contrasts the righteousness of the Pharisees and the expectant righteousness of His followers in verse 20. Match the people with their best description.

Scribes and Pharisees	Concerned only with following the letter of the Law, external obedience only, bare minimum
Jesus's followers	Concerned also with the spirit of the law, internal obedience, heart that matches deeds

7. (I) Paraphrase in one sentence the main point Jesus is making in verses 19–20.

   _____

   _____

   _____

8. (T) How are you tempted to relax the true intent of God's law?

   _____

   _____

   _____

Day 5: Read Matthew 5:21-48

Verses 21-48

1. (I,T) Fill in the chart below with the six illustrations Jesus uses to reveal "righteousness that exceeds that of the scribes and Pharisees." The first one has been completed for you.

	What they heard: Was it a true or false Statement?	What is the letter of the law? (external obedience)	Have you ever broken this law?	What is the spirit of the law? (internal)) The reason for the law	Have you ever broken this "law"?	Inner virtue/ righteousness His teaching develops
Matthew 21-26	(Read Exodus 20:13) What they heard was a true statement	Do not murder	No, I have never murdered anyone	Unrighteous anger, hatred, contempt	Yes	Peacemaking
Matthew 27-30	(Read Exodus 20:14)					
Matthew 31-32	(Read Deuteronomy 24:1-4)					
Matthew 33-37	(Read Numbers 30:2)					

	What they heard: Was it a true or false Statement?	What is the letter of the law? (external obedience)	Have you ever broken this law?	What is the spirit of the law? (internal)) The reason for the law	Have you ever broken this "law"?	Inner virtue/ righteousness His teaching develops
Matthew 38-42	(Read Exodus 21:24)					
Matthew 43-48	(Read Leviticus 19:18)					

2. (I) Summarize Jesus's overall message in this section.

_____

_____

_____

_____

3. (I) What is Jesus's attitude regarding obedience?

_____

_____

_____

_____

4.   (T) Which virtue are you lacking most that the Holy Spirit needs to grow within you?

_____

_____

_____

5.   (I) Paraphrase verse 48. Read the following verses to help: Zechariah 4:6, Romans 3:22-24, 2 Corinthians 5:21, Ephesians 4:13, 22-24.

_____

_____

_____

6.   (T) What is your response to Jesus's words in these verses? Be specific. In what ways has the Holy Spirit convicted you this week or prompted deeper obedience in your life?

_____

_____

_____

_____

Day 6: Commit what you learned to prayer. Reread Matthew 5.

Adoration:

"God, you are…."

Pray the attributes of God we studied this week back to God.

Confession:

"Lord, I confess…."

In light of the above and what we studied this week, what did you learn about yourself?

Thanksgiving:

"Thank you…."

What from this week's passage made your heart overflow with thanksgiving?

Supplication:

"I lift up…."

After reading this week's passage, what petitions do you need to ask of God?

Global: _____

Local: _____

Personal: _____

MATTHEW 6-7

God Gives Godly Wisdom to His Children

AIM: God gives godly wisdom to His children.

Scripture to Memorize:

But seek first the kingdom of God and His righteousness, and all these things will be added to you.

—Matt. 6:33

Attribute of God: Wise

God always knows what is best. His Word is full of His wisdom. All wisdom is a gift from God and like the wise men, to be wise, we must seek Him. Since God is the only one who is truly and perfectly wise, He alone deserves the honor and glory in all things. We as creatures must always be growing and learning, but God does acquire wisdom. His wisdom defines who He is. He is wise. We can look to the cross to see the wisdom of God on display in Christ.

Doctrine: The Bible

The Bible is a book comprised of 66 different books. It includes about 40 different earthly authors and was written over a period of about 1500 years. It is divided into two main sections where 39 books make up the Old Testament and 27 books make up the New Testament. Its unified theme is because it is ultimately written by one author – God – who inspired all the earthly authors. Scripture is the very words of God spoken to us through these authors. God could have chosen to reveal Himself in any way He wanted, but chose to reveal Himself in a tangible expression through human language. The Bible explains who God is, what He has done for us, and His plans and purposes for all humankind. Jesus is the main character in the Bible - the whole book is about Him. In the Old Testament, He is predicted and anticipated, and in the New Testament He is revealed and preached. The Bible exposes the world's brokenness, how sin came to be in the world, and how God's Son came to reverse the curse and restore all things. The Bible, through the power of the Holy Spirit, shines a light in the darkness of our hearts and reveals our need for a Savior.   -

The Bible is more than just merely a book. It is alive and active and able to transform hearts. It is good for us to read, study, memorize, and meditate on. It teaches us, rebukes (or corrects) us, sanctifies us and gives instructions on how to live a righteous life. It is the education for all disciples of Jesus Christ. It is the main way God grows His children spiritually. It has the power to unite, but also divide truth from error. The Bible is God's gift to us, and we should never take for granted the special privilege some of us have in owning our very own Bible.

Day 1: Read Matthew 6-7

1. In two to three sentences, summarize what happens in these chapters.

    Chapter 6

    _____

    _____

    _____

    Chapter 7

    _____

    _____

    _____

2. What part of the Sermon on the Mount do you find most encouraging? Most convicting? Most surprising?

    _____

    _____

    _____

    _____

Day 2: Read Matthew 6:1-15

Verse 1

1. (I) Compare 6:1 to 5:16 from last week. Do these verses contradict each other? Explain your answer.

_____

_____

_____

Verses 2-4

2. (E) What is the first religious act Jesus spotlights (v. 2)?

"Thus, when you _____."

_____

_____

_____

3. (E) What motivates the hypocrites' actions in verse 2? What is their reward?

_____

_____

_____

4. (E,I) What or who motivates a disciple's actions in verse 4? Or who is their reward? (See Genesis 15:1 in the New International Version (NIV) to help with your answer.)

_____

_____

_____

_____

5. (I) What do you think Jesus's main concern is in verses 2-4?

_____

_____

_____

6. (T) How do you see this happening in churches today?

_____

_____

_____

_____

Verses 5-8

7. (E) What is the second religious act Jesus spotlights (v. 5)?

    "And, when you _____."

8. (E) What motivates the hypocrites' actions in verse 5? What is their reward?

_____

_____

_____

_____

9. (E,I) What or who motivates a disciple's actions in verse 6? What or who is their reward? (See Revelation 21:3 to help with the answer.)

_____

_____

_____

_____

10. (I) What do you think Jesus's main concern is in verses 5-8?

_____

_____

_____

_____

11. (T) How does the truth that God "is in secret" and "sees in secret" encourage you? Challenge you?

_____

_____

_____

_____

Verses 9-15

12. (I) The Lord's Prayer is broken into two sections. Mark which section is focused vertically (upward) and which is focused horizontally (outward). Why is this important to note?

9-10

_____

_____

_____

_____

11-13

_____

_____

_____

_____

13. (I) Write the letter next to each phrase of the Lord's Prayer that corresponds to its closely related description.

Our _____	a. Confession and repentance of our sin against God
Father _____	b. Petition for physical and spiritual provision
In heaven _____	c. A believer's desire is to hate sin and turn from it
Hallowed be your name _____	d. We forgive others because Christ has forgiven us
Your Kingdom come, Your will be done _____	e. Intended for community prayer
On earth as it is in heaven _____	f. Present and future fulfillment
Give us this day our daily bread _____	g. Petition for Your name to be revered as holy
And forgive us our debts _____	h. Submission to Your plans and purposes
As we also have forgiven our debtors _____	i. Near and accessible
And lead us not into temptation _____	j. Jesus delivers us from our sins
But deliver us from evil _____	k. Transcendent, superior

14. (T) Jesus said our willingness to forgive or not forgive is directly tied to our understanding of our own forgiveness given by the Father. How can forgiving others give us a deeper understanding of the Gospel message? How can this truth change your relationships?

_____

_____

_____

Day 3: Read Matthew 6:16-34

Verses 16-18

1. (E) What is the third religious act Jesus spotlights (v. 16)?

   "And, when you _____."

2. (E) What motivates the hypocrites' actions in verse 16? What is their reward?

   _____

   _____

   _____

3. (E,I) What or who motivates a disciple's actions in verse 18? What or who is their reward?

   _____

   _____

   _____

4. (I) What do you think Jesus's main concern is in these verses?

   _____

   _____

   _____

   _____

5. (T) How did these verses change your prior ideas about fasting (if they did)? What actions can you take in light of this truth?

   _____

   _____

   _____

   _____

Verses 19-23

6. (I) Place either temporary or eternal in each blank.

    vv. 19-21

    Treasures on earth   _____

    Treasures in heaven   _____

    vv. 22-23

    Eyes fixed on earthly things   _____

    Eyes fixed on Jesus   _____

    v. 24

    Serving God   _____

    Serving money/material wealth   _____

7. (I) What does Jesus want to communicate to His followers?

    _____

    _____

    _____

    _____

    _____

8. (T) What earthly distractions steal your attention from heavenly treasures? What do your thoughts, money, and priorities reveal about what you treasure most?

    _____

    _____

    _____

    _____

    _____

Verses 25-34

9. (I) What is *therefore* in verse 25 "there for"? What idea is it connecting from the previous section (vv. 19-24)?

_____

_____

_____

10. (E) How many times does Jesus use the word *anxious* in this section? List the specific things Jesus told us to not worry about.

_____

_____

_____

11. (I) Explain how faith and worry are connected in these verses.

_____

_____

_____

12. (I) Explain how our view of God diminishes when we are anxious.

_____

_____

_____

13. (E) What is God's remedy for worry (v. 33)?

_____

_____

_____

14. (I) List the attributes of God that are highlighted in this section. One has been done for you.

Accessible

_____

_____

_____

15. (T) What causes you to be anxious? Will you surrender it to God today?

_____

_____

_____

Day 4: Read Matthew 7:1-12

Verses 1-6

1. (E) Look up the word *judge* (verb) in a dictionary and write the definition below.

_____

_____

_____

2. (E) Look up 7:3 in the NIV. What two objects are used?

"Why do you look at the speck of _____ in your brother's eye and pay no attention to the _____ in your own eye?"

_____

_____

_____

_____

3. (E,I) Jesus uses two objects made from the same substance but varying in size. Who has the larger object? Who has the smaller object? What point is Jesus trying to make?

    _____

    _____

    _____

4. (I) Why is self-examination so important before examining someone else (James 2:12-13)?

    _____

    _____

    _____

    _____

5. (I) Read the following verses and note the main thought.

    James 5:19-20

    _____

    _____

    _____

    Galatians 6:1-5

    _____

    _____

    _____

    Ephesians 4:2

    _____

    _____

    _____

6. (T) What type of judging is Jesus warning us not to do?

_____

_____

_____

7. (I) What is the difference between this kind of wrong judgment Jesus is describing and wise discernment (Hebrews 5:14)?

_____

_____

_____

8. (T) Do you tend to judge others harshly and hypocritically? In what way?

_____

_____

_____

9. (T) How can fellow believers help one another in their struggle with sin in a loving and discerning way?

_____

_____

_____

10. (E,I) What is the holy pearl Jesus is referring to (Matthew 13:45-46)? Paraphrase verse 6.

_____

_____

_____

_____

11. (I) How does verse 6 relate to verses 1-5?

_____

_____

_____

_____

Verses 7-12

12. (E) List the three descriptions of prayer in these verses and each of God's promises when you pray this way.

_____

_____

_____

_____

13. (I) Does this mean God grants whatever we ask (Proverbs 28:9)?

_____

_____

_____

_____

14. (T) There are "good things" our heavenly Father will always grant His children when they ask. What do you think a Kingdom citizen asks, seeks, and knocks for? (Think back to chapters 5 and 6.)

_____

_____

_____

_____

15. (I) Where is the emphasis in these verses—on the Father or the child? On the giver or the receiver? What do these verses reveal to us about God?

_____

_____

_____

16. (T) What do you ask for regularly? How will your findings above change the way you pray?

_____

_____

_____

17. (I) The word *so* at the beginning of verse 12 is connecting a logical thought. How does verse 12 connect with verses 7-11?

_____

_____

_____

18. (I) How does the Golden Rule (v. 12) summarize all the teachings of the Law and the Prophets?

_____

_____

_____

Day 5: Read Matthew 7:13-29

Verses 13-27

1. (E,I) Fill in the chart by summarizing the contrasting images Jesus uses in His sermon conclusion.

Contrasting characteristics		
	Two Kinds	Eternal Fate
Gates	(vv. 13–14) Narrow – hard and few find it Wide – easy and majority enter it	Narrow – life Wide – destruction
Teachers	(vv. 15–20)	
Disciples/ Followers	(vv. 21–23)	
Builders	(vv. 24–27)	
Foundations	(vv. 24–27)	

2. (I) What reveals the type of foundation the house is built on?

   _____

   _____

   _____

3. (T) How does this truth change your perspective about the "storms of life"?

    _____

    _____

    _____

4. (T) In what ways do your findings from the chart challenge our current culture?

    _____

    _____

    _____

5. (T) What warning or convictions do these passages have for you personally?

    _____

    _____

    _____

6. (E) What tool did God give us that is essential in discerning the two kinds of gates, the two kind of teachers, the two kinds of followers, good and evil, right and wrong? (See Acts 17:11, Hebrews 4:12, and the doctrine this week.)

    _____

    _____

    _____

Verses 28-29

7. (E) How did the crowd respond to Jesus's teaching? Why did they respond this way?

    _____

    _____

    _____

Day 6: Commit what you learned to prayer. Reread Matthew 6-7.

Adoration:

"God, you are…."

Pray the attributes of God we studied this week back to God.

Confession:

"Lord, I confess…."

In light of the above and what we studied this week, what did you learn about yourself?

Thanksgiving:

"Thank you…."

What from this week's passage made your heart overflow with thanksgiving?

Supplication:

"I lift up…."

After reading this week's passage, what petitions do you need to ask from God?

Global: _____

Local: _____

Personal: _____

MATTHEW 8-10

Jesus's Mercy Is Greater Than All Our Sins

AIM: Jesus's mercy is greater than all our sins.

Scripture to Memorize:

When he saw the crowds, he had compassion for them, because they were harassed and helpless, like sheep without a shepherd.

–Matt. 9:36

Attribute of God: Compassionate

God cares for His children and acts on their behalf. It is one of the major themes throughout the entire Bible. It includes the overwhelming distress one feels on behalf of another from deep within and moves to action to seek to alleviate the distress out of love. God's compassion is bottomless and endless. He is sympathetic to our weaknesses and hears us when we cry out to Him. Jesus is the full embodiment of compassion and our perfect model to follow.

Doctrine: Faith

The Bible defines faith as "assurance of things hoped for, the conviction of things not seen" (Hebrews 11:1). Faith goes beyond just wishful thinking or having a positive optimistic outlook. Biblical faith involves substance. It is belief in something and extends to a wholehearted trust. Even a person who does not consider themselves "religious" still has faith. An atheist has faith, it is just a misplaced faith. The reason that it is accurate to place your faith in Christ is because He alone is perfectly good and perfectly trustworthy. We cannot place our faith on anything earthly such as money, presidents, doctors, our spouse, or even pastors. These things keep our focus on temporary, imperishable, and circumstantial things. These things will give us a shaky, unstable foundation. Only faith in God keeps our eyes fixed on him and on things that are eternal and everlasting and give us sure, solid rock foundation. Faith is the core essential, the only means to salvation. One cannot be saved without faith and this faith is a trust in God—who He is and what He has done. It goes beyond just mere acknowledgement to a commitment.

Faith is a gift and is not the result of anything we have done or achieved. God has to initiate the relationship, and then we respond "in faith." Even though our actions do not provide the means of salvation, it is the result or fruit of faith. Saving faith always results in action. Faith and good deeds have always been linked. They are different sides to the same coin. Our good works are proof that our faith is alive. We reveal our faith in Christ by our trust that is revealed through our actions. In Scripture, the disciples were often characterized by little faith, but Jesus was always teaching it is not the size of our faith, but who we place our faith in that ultimately matters. God can and will grow our faith. But, it does mean giving up any false sense of control we thought we may have had in our life and trusting the Creator of the World in all things. This is faith.

Day 1: Read Matthew 8-10

1. In two to three sentences, summarize what happens in these chapters.

Chapter 8

_____

_____

_____

Chapter 9

_____

_____

_____

Chapter 10

_____

_____

_____

2. How is God's glory still evident in circumstances where individuals do not receive a physical healing?

_____

_____

_____

Day 2: Read Matthew 8:1-15

Verses 1-4

1. (I) Was this man with leprosy considered ceremonially clean or unclean (Leviticus 13:1-3)?

_____

_____

_____

2. (E) Read Leviticus 13:45-46 and 15:31. Note what life would have been like for a person with leprosy.

_____

_____

_____

3. (I) What does the touch in verse 3 reveal about Jesus?

_____

_____

_____

4. (E) How was the man cleansed of his leprosy? Fill in the blanks.

"And Jesus stretched out His hand and touched him, _____, 'I will; _____.' And immediately his leprosy was cleansed."

5. (E) What did Jesus require of the man who was healed (v. 4)?

_____

_____

_____

6. (E) What did Jesus mean when He said to "offer the gift that Moses commanded"? (Read Leviticus 14:4–7 to help with your answer.)

_____

_____

_____

7. (E) Why does it say Jesus wanted this man to go and make the sacrifice?

_____

_____

_____

8. (I) What kind of restorations would this man experience now that he is cleansed?

_____

_____

_____

_____

9. (T) How is this a picture of our own restoration in Christ Jesus?

_____

_____

_____

_____

10. (T) How do you tend to respond when someone is healed of sickness? How can these verses change the way you view healings?

_____

_____

_____

Verses 5-13

11. (E) Is the centurion a Jew or a Gentile?

_____

_____

_____

12. (E,I) Who did the centurion want to be healed? What does this reveal about the centurion?

_____

_____

_____

13. (E) What was Jesus's response to the centurion in verse 7?

_____

_____

_____

14. (I) Why might the centurion respond as he did to Jesus in verse 8? (Read Acts 10:28 to help with the answer.)

_____

_____

_____

15. (I) Review your answer from question 14. How does Jesus's response in verse 7 break this tradition? How does this speak to His mission from Matthew 4:12-17?

_____

_____

_____

16. (I) What else does verse 8 reveal about the centurion? What name does he call Jesus?

_____

_____

_____

17. (E,I) Summarize what the centurion is saying in verse 9.

_____

_____

_____

18. (I) Why would Jesus commend this kind of faith (v. 10)?

_____

_____

_____

19. (I) In what way does Jesus's teaching in verses 11-12 connect to John's rebuke of the Pharisees and Sadducees in 3:9? What is Jesus's point in verses 11-12? (Read Isaiah 60:3-4 to help with your answer.)

_____

_____

_____

20. (E) What is the place Jesus is referring to in verse 12?

_____

_____

_____

21. (E) How was the centurion's servant healed of his suffering? Fill in the blanks.

"And to the centurion Jesus said, 'Go; _____ for you as you have believed.' And the servant was healed at that very moment."

22. (T) What lessons can you learn from the centurion, and how can you apply them to your daily life?

_____

_____

_____

Verses 14–15

23. (E) Was the third person Jesus healed a man or a woman?

_____

_____

_____

_____

24. (I) What does the healing of Peter's mother-in-law reveal to us about Jesus's heart?

_____

_____

_____

_____

25. (E) What did she do immediately after she was healed?

_____

_____

_____

26. (I) Look up the word *authority* in a dictionary and write a definition for it below that best fits the context of what you read.

_____

_____

_____

27. (E) Circle the correct phrase that goes with verses 1–15.

Jesus has authority over sickness and disease.

Jesus has authority over nature.

Jesus has authority over Satan and the demonic world.

Jesus has authority over death and chaos.

28. (I) Find two verses or passages in the Old Testament where God demonstrates His authority in the same way you circled above, and list them below.

_____

_____

_____

29. (I) Write your answers to questions 1, 11, and 23 below. What do you think is significant about Matthew putting these healings in this order and as the first three healings? (Hint: think about the Old Testament temple structure.)

_____

_____

_____

30. (T) How does Jesus Christ offer full access to all those who come to Him in faith? How does that encourage you today?

_____

_____

_____

Day 3: Read Matthew 8:16-34

Verses 16-17

1. (I) Read Isaiah 53:4-5. How does this prophecy find fulfillment in Jesus Christ?

_____

_____

_____

Verses 18-22

2. (E,T) Fill in the chart below.

	What They Said	How Jesus Responded
Verses 19-20	Scribe:	
Verses 21-22	Disciple:	

3. (T) One man was over-eager in following Jesus, thinking it would be a life of ease. One man was under-eager in following Jesus due to a divided heart. Both illustrate the cost of following Jesus. Give examples of modern-day responses that reveal someone's reluctance to completely and immediately follow Jesus Christ.

_____

_____

_____

4. (I) Does verse 20 contradict what we learned in Matthew 6 about how God's children should trust Him as their provider and not worry about life's basic needs? Explain your answer.

_____

_____

_____

5. (T) Think about your own personal response to Jesus's call. Can you relate to the two mentioned above in the chart? How has submitting to Jesus's authority been worth the cost?

_____

_____

_____

_____

Verses 23-27

6. (E) Who was with Jesus in the boat?

_____

_____

_____

_____

7. (E) What was Jesus doing in verse 24?

_____

_____

_____

_____

8. (E) How did the disciples respond to the storm in verse 25?

_____

_____

_____

_____

9. (E) What is Jesus's response to the disciples' fear in verse 26?

_____

_____

_____

_____

10. (I) How are faith and fear connected?

_____

_____

_____

_____

11. (E) Fill in the blanks from verse 26.

"Then, He rose and _____ the winds and the sea, and there was a great _____."

12. (E,I) What was the response of the disciples in verse 27? Compare that to verse 25. What changed?

_____

_____

_____

13. (E) Circle the correct phrase that goes with verses 23-27.

Jesus has authority over sickness and disease.

Jesus has authority over nature.

Jesus has authority over Satan and the demonic world.

Jesus has authority over death and chaos.

14. (I) Find two verses or passages in the Old Testament where God demonstrates His authority in the same way you circled above, and list them below.

_____

_____

_____

15. (I) How do these verses reveal both Jesus's humanity and deity?

_____

_____

_____

16. (T) Describe a time God put you through a "storm." What was it? How did God use it to grow your faith? How did that storm give God the glory?

_____

_____

_____

_____

Verses 28-34

17. (E) Who did Jesus meet in verse 28?

_____

_____

_____

18. (E) Fill in the blanks from verse 29. What did they cry out?

"And behold, they cried out, 'What have you to do with us, O _____ of _____?'

19. (I) What does this reveal about the demons? (Read James 2:19 to help with your answer.)

_____

_____

_____

20. (E) Fill in the blanks from verse 32.

"And He _____ to them, _____. So they _____ and _____ into the pigs."

21. (I) Circle the correct phrase that goes with verses 28-32.

Jesus has authority over sickness and disease.

Jesus has authority over nature.

Jesus has authority over Satan and the demonic world.

Jesus has authority over death and chaos.

22. (I) Find two verses or passages in the Old Testament where God demonstrates His authority in the same way you circled above, and list them below.

_____

_____

_____

23. (T) What did you learn about Jesus's power and authority? How will that impact your life this week?

_____

_____

_____

Day 4: Read Matthew 9

Verses 1-8

1. (E) Fill in the blanks from verse 2.

   "And when Jesus saw their faith, he _____ to the paralytic, 'Take heart, my son; _____.'"

2. (I) Circle the correct phrase that goes with verse 2.

   Jesus has authority over sickness and disease.

   Jesus has authority over nature.

   Jesus has authority over Satan and the demonic world.

   Jesus has authority over death and chaos.

   Jesus has authority to forgive and remove sin.

3. (I) Find two verses or passages in the Old Testament where God demonstrates His authority in the same way you circled above. List them below.

   _____

   _____

   _____

4. (I) Is this an external healing or an internal healing?

   _____

   _____

   _____

5. (E) What was the response of the scribes and Pharisees?

_____

_____

_____

6. (I) What attribute of Jesus do we see in verse 4?

_____

_____

_____

7. (T) Which do you truly believe is the greater miracle? A changed heart (internal healing) or a paralytic man walking (external healing)?

_____

_____

_____

8. (I) In what ways does the physical miracle (lesser) point to the spiritual miracle (greater)?

_____

_____

_____

_____

9. (I) Summarize Jesus's main point in verses 1-6.

_____

_____

_____

_____

10. (T) How does our culture today still crave the seen over the unseen?

_____

_____

_____

11. (E) What was the crowd's response to the paralytic man standing and walking?

_____

_____

_____

12. (T) Reflect on what it means for you personally that Jesus has the power and authority to say, "Your sins are forgiven."

_____

_____

_____

Verses 9-13

13. (E) Fill in the blanks from verse 9.

"As Jesus passed on from there, he saw a man called _____ sitting at the tax booth, and He _____ to Him, 'Follow me.' And he _____ and _____ him."

14. (I) Why do you think Matthew incorporated his own call in the narratives of Jesus's miracles and healings?

_____

_____

_____

_____

15. (E) What was Jesus doing with the tax collectors and sinners in verse 10?

_____

_____

_____

_____

16. (E,I) What do the Pharisees call Jesus in verse 11? What does that reveal about them?

_____

_____

_____

17. (E) What did the Pharisees ask Jesus's disciples in verse 11?

_____

_____

_____

18. (E,I) What was Jesus's response to the Pharisees in verse 12? How would that have been an admonition to them?

_____

_____

_____

19. (I) Verse 13 says, "I desire mercy, and not sacrifice." It is a quote from Hosea 6:6. The same principal can be found in 1 Samuel 15:22. What do you think this means? (Refer back to the chart in Chapter 5, Day 5.)

_____

_____

_____

20. (T) How are we often guilty of the same thinking as the Pharisees? How can this truth change you?

_____

_____

_____

Verses 14-17

21. (E,I) These verses are filled with Old Testament language. How do these parables point us to the "new" things Jesus provides? Read the following verses to help with your answer.

Isaiah 61:10
Jeremiah 31:31-33
Ezekiel 36:26-27
Zechariah 3:4
Matthew 5:17
Luke 22:20
Romans 6:14-23
Galatians 3:28
2 Corinthians 5:17
Hebrews 8:6
Revelation 19:8

22. (I) In two to three sentences, summarize Jesus's main point in verses 14-17.

_____

_____

_____

Verses 20-22

23. (I) What problem did the woman in verse 20 have? Describe what her life would have been like (Leviticus 15).

_____

_____

24. (E) Fill in the blanks from verse 22.

"Jesus turned, and seeing her he, _____, 'Take heart, _____, your faith has made you well.' And _____ the woman was _____."

25. (E,T) What familial term did Jesus use with the woman? How does that encourage you?

_____

_____

_____

Verses 18-19, 23-26

26. (E) What problem did the ruler have in verse 18? What did he ask of Jesus?

_____

_____

27. (E) Describe the scene in the ruler's house when Jesus got there.

_____

_____

28. (E) How did Jesus heal the girl in verse 25?

_____

_____

29. (I) Circle the correct phrase that goes with these verses.

Jesus has authority over sickness and disease.

Jesus has authority over nature.

Jesus has authority over Satan and the demonic world.

Jesus has authority over death and chaos.

30. (I) Find two verses or passages in the Old Testament where God demonstrates His authority in the same way you circled above. List them below.

_____

_____

_____

Verses 27-31

31. (E) What were these two men's problems? What did they call Jesus in verse 27? (Read 2 Samuel 7:12-16 for further understanding of this title.)

_____

_____

_____

32. (E) Fill in the blank from verse 30.

"And their _____."

33. (E) What did Jesus ask of them in verse 30? Did the men obey or disobey?

_____

_____

_____

Verses 32-34

34. (E) What was the man's problem in verse 32?

_____

_____

_____

35. (E) Fill in the blanks from verse 33.

    "And when the demon had been cast out, the _____."

36. (I) How are these healings from this chapter a fulfillment of Isaiah 35:3-6? How are these healings a fitting end to Matthew's account of Jesus's healings?

    _____

    _____

    _____

37. (E,I) What is the response of the Pharisees in verse 34? What does that reveal about them?

    _____

    _____

    _____

38. (I) Jesus healed people who demonstrated great faith, little faith, and no faith. He healed when they asked and even when they didn't. He healed those who obeyed and those who did not. What does this teach us about faith in relation to healings? Why is this significant?

    _____

    _____

    _____

    _____

39. (T) How does this teaching differ from what the prosperity Gospel teaches?

    _____

    _____

    _____

    _____

Verses 35–38

40. (I) Compare verse 35 to 4:23. What do you notice?

_____

_____

_____

41. (E) How did Jesus describe the crowd in verse 36?

_____

_____

_____

42. (I) Match the metaphor to the person(s) it represents.

The harvest   Jesus

The laborers   Those who share the Gospel

Lord of the harvest   Lost souls

43. (T) How does this title of Christ help us understand His role in evangelism?

_____

_____

_____

_____

44. (E) What are Jesus's disciples instructed to pray for in verse 38?

_____

_____

_____

_____

45. (T) How is this prayer just as urgent today? How can you practically obey this command of God?

_____

_____

_____

Day 5: Read Matthew 10

Verses 1-4

1. (I,T) Compare 9:39 to 10:1. Who was the answer to the disciples' prayer? What can you learn from this?

_____

_____

_____

2. (E) List the 12 apostles below.

_____

_____

_____

_____

Verses 5-15

3. (E,I) Where were the apostles instructed to go? Why do you think this is (Isaiah 60:3, Genesis 12:3, Romans 1:16)?

_____

_____

_____

_____

4. (E,I) Compare 9:35 to 10:5-8. Are they the same or different? Who did it first? Why would this be encouraging for the apostles?

_____

_____

_____

_____

5. (T) Give some examples of how you could follow the command to proclaim the message of the Kingdom "as you go" in your daily life?

_____

_____

_____

_____

6. (E,I) What other instructions were the apostles given in verses 9-10? Why do you think they were instructed this way? (Review Matthew 6:25-33.)

_____

_____

_____

_____

7. (E) What were the apostles' instructions to the house or town that received the message of the Kingdom? To the house or town that did not receive it?

_____

_____

_____

_____

_____

8. (T) Read Genesis 19 for the story of Sodom and Gomorrah. Jesus mentions that it will be more bearable on the day of judgment for these ancient cities than the house or town that rejected His message from the apostles. (Read Luke 12:47-48 and Hebrews 10:26-29 for further understanding.) What do you learn from this? How is this a warning for you? How is this a comfort to you?

    _____

    _____

    _____

Verses 16-25

9. (I) Jesus gives warnings to His disciples. Are these warnings written as an "if" they happen or a "when" they happen?

    _____

    _____

    _____

10. (E,I) In Matthew 10:16, Jesus used an analogy with four animals. List the four animals and your best guess of what each one symbolizes. Summarize Jesus's overall message to His disciples.

    _____

    _____

    _____

11. (E,T) In 10:17-18, Jesus prophesies three events that are fulfilled in the book of Acts. List the three acts of persecution that will come to His disciples. What does that reveal to us about Jesus? What does that teach us about the life of a follower of Christ?

    _____

    _____

    _____

12. (E) Jesus gives more warnings of the persecution that is to come but also offers comfort to His disciples. List each encouraging promise.

Verses 19–20

_____

_____

Verse 22

_____

_____

Verse 24

_____

_____

13. (T) Have you ever been given the right words at the right time to defend your faith? Describe that time in the space below.

_____

_____

_____

_____

_____

14. (T) Which promise from these verses is particularly meaningful to you? Why?

_____

_____

_____

_____

_____

Verses 26-33

15. (E,I) What connecting word is used at the beginning of verse 26? How do these verses build on the previous verses?

_____

_____

_____

_____

16. (I) Who are "those" who can kill the body but not the soul? Who is "him" who can destroy both body and soul?

_____

_____

_____

_____

17. (I,T) Paraphrase verse 28. How are these words still true today (Deuteronomy 10:12-13, Proverbs 1:7, Ecclesiastes 12:13)?

_____

_____

_____

_____

_____

18. (I) In verses 29-31, Jesus comforts His disciples. Match the phrase on the left with the truth it is communicating.

Not even sparrows sold for a penny will fall to the ground apart from your Father   You are known

Even the hairs on your head are numbered   You are valued

19. (I) How would knowing this help rightly orient the disciples' focus?

_____

_____

_____

20. (I) What eternal significance are verses 32-33 expressing?

_____

_____

_____

21. (I) What attributes of God do you see in these verses?

_____

_____

_____

22. (T) How are you tempted to wrongly fear mankind? How can you turn this fear into a right and reverent fear of the Lord?

_____

_____

_____

Verses 34-39

23. (E) Jesus teaches Kingdom above family. He uses the sword to illustrate that His Gospel message will bring division. List all the familial relationships that Jesus says His message will divide.

_____

_____

_____

24. (I) Notice that the relationship between a husband and a wife is not mentioned. Why do you think that is?

_____

_____

_____

25. (T) In what ways have your personally seen Christ's message, "Bring a sword"?

_____

_____

_____

26. (I) Jesus then teaches Kingdom above self. Paraphrase verses 38-39.

_____

_____

_____

27. (T) What does this look like in your own life?

_____

_____

_____

Verses 40-42

28. Jesus ends on a positive note with the idea of reward. We spoke of rewards in Matthew 6. How is that same idea in these verses (Genesis 15:1 NIV)?

_____

_____

_____

29. (T) How can you be about the business of Kingdom ministry? What would it look like for you to "give a cup of cold water" to a fellow Christian as they are ministering?

_____

_____

_____

Day 6: Commit what you learned to prayer. Reread Matthew 8-10.

Adoration:

"God, you are…."

Pray the attributes of God we studied this week back to God.

Confession:

"Lord, I confess…."

In light of the above and what we studied this week, what did you learn about yourself?

Thanksgiving:

"Thank you…."

What from this week's passage made your heart overflow with thanksgiving?

Supplication:

"I lift up…."

After reading this week's passage, what petitions do you need to ask of God?

Global: _____

Local: _____

Personal: _____

MATTHEW 11–13

Jesus Is the Better Temple

AIM: Jesus is the better temple.

Scripture to Memorize:

For whoever does the will of my Father in heaven is my brother and sister and mother.

–Matt. 12:50

Attribute of God: Just

God cannot over punish or under punish. His judgments are always fair. He shows no partiality or favoritism and perfectly administers a verdict for each crime. It would be unjust for God to ignore sin or look the other way, but because of what Jesus did for us on the cross by suffering the full punishment of sin, justice was satisfied once and for all. This is how justice can be fully satisfied, and a sinner be saved at the same time. Jesus is just and the Justifier by being the sacrifice that satisfied the demands of God's wrath.

Doctrine: Judgment of Believers and Unbelievers

One great truth found in Scripture is that one day all will meet our Creator and when we do, every person who has ever lived will be judged. God will be the just judge because He knows everything about everyone and will be able to provide a verdict that is unbiased, just, and fair. However, it can go one of two ways. The good news for those who trust in Christ for salvation will not be found guilty or fall under any condemnation because their sin has already been paid for on the cross. In Christ, God satisfied His wrath and punished His perfect Son in our place. Believers will only be appraised for their service to Christ while on Earth and will spend all eternity in the presence of the Lord.

Unbelievers, however, will carry the weight of their own sin and will face eternal punishment in hell. All unbelievers are storing up God's wrath because all sin must be punished. Many may be uncomfortable with the thought of hell, but to ignore the reality of it is to actually make yourself God and place yourself in the Judge's seat. Even under human law, a person who commits a crime must be punished. How much more so when one commits an offense and transgression against a holy God? This is why we must share the Gospel with others.

God judges a person not from any external appearances, but from the inside. He has the ability to look within a person and know their true character. God looks at the heart. And only a heart that has been changed and transformed by the indwelling of the Holy Spirit will be saved.

Day 1: Read Matthew 11-13

1. In two to three sentences, summarize what happens in these chapters.

Chapter 11

_____

_____

_____

_____

Chapter 12

_____

_____

_____

_____

Chapter 13

_____

_____

_____

_____

2. How would you explain the kingdom of heaven to an unbeliever?

_____

_____

_____

Day 2: Read Matthew 11

Verses 1-6

1. Fill in the blanks.

   "When Jesus had finished instructing his _____, He _____ from there to _____ and _____ in _____."

2. (E,I) Where was John the Baptist in verse 2? What did he ask Jesus by way of His disciples (v. 3)? Why do you think John was questioning if Jesus was the "one who is to come"?

   _____

   _____

   _____

   _____

3. What does this reveal about John concerning his trust in God?

   _____

   _____

   _____

   _____

4. (E) How did Jesus reply to John's doubt? Fill in the blanks.

   "Go and tell John what you _____ and _____."

5. (E) List the evidence of Jesus's words (what's been heard) and deeds (what's been seen) that the disciples witnessed (v. 5).

_____

_____

_____

_____

6. (I) How is Jesus the fulfillment of Isaiah 35:5-6 and Isaiah 61:1? How would this have been reassuring to John?

_____

_____

_____

_____

7. (T) When have your life circumstances caused you to doubt? How does meditating on God's Word provide the best answer to our doubts?

_____

_____

_____

_____

Verses 7-15

8. (I,T) Is Jesus commending or rebuking John and his ministry in these verses? What can you learn from this, especially just after John's expression of doubt?

_____

_____

_____

_____

9. (I) How is John the Baptist the fulfillment of Malachi 3:1-4 and 4:5-6?

_____

_____

_____

10. (I) Paraphrase verse 11. (Use 1 Peter 1:10-11 to help.)

_____

_____

_____

11. (I) How does confirming John's identity as the prophesied prophet confirm Jesus's own identity to the people?

_____

_____

_____

Verses 16-19

12. (E,I) What transition word begins verse 16? What transition or switching over is Jesus making?

_____

_____

_____

13. (E) What word does Jesus use to describe "this generation" in verse 16?

_____

_____

_____

THE GOSPEL ACCORDING TO MATTHEW

14. (E,I) Compare verses 18 and 19.

    (circle one)

    John the Baptist (did) (did not) come eating and drinking (v. 18).

    What did "they" say about him (v. 18)?

    (circle one)

    Jesus (did) (did not) come eating and drinking (v. 19).

    What did "they" call him (v. 19)?

15. (E) Who most likely are "they" in these verses (see Matthew 9:11)?

    _____

    _____

    _____

16. (I) Verse 19 in the NIV sums up this section when it says that "wisdom is proved right by her deeds." Place the verse number from this section next to each way the religious leaders showed their lack of wisdom.

    _____   spiritual pride

    _____   childish; determined not to be pleased

    _____   failure to recognize the forerunner to the Messiah

    _____   failure to recognize the Messiah and His Kingdom

    _____   wrongly critical and inconsistent in their judgments

17. (T) Has pride ever hardened your heart that resulted in sinning in a way similar to the religious leaders? Describe it in the space below.

    _____

    _____

    _____

    _____

    _____

Verses 20-24

18. (I) Read Ezekiel 28:10 and Genesis 19:1-9. Note what the historical cities of Tyre, Sidon, and Sodom were condemned and known for.

_____

_____

_____

_____

19. (E) In verses 20-23, Jesus condemns His modern-day cities of Chorazin, Bethsaida, and Capernaum. What had Jesus done there? What did they fail to do? (v.20)

_____

_____

_____

_____

20. (E) Which cities will receive a greater judgment – the historical cities or the modern day cities?

_____

_____

_____

_____

21. (I) How do these verses (20-24) reiterate the same idea as Matthew 10:14-15 (see Hebrews 10:26 and Luke 12:47-48)? Why will some cities receive a greater judgment than others?

_____

_____

_____

_____

22. (I) What attribute(s) of God do we learn from these verses?

_____

_____

_____

23. (T) How seriously does Jesus take the sin of indifference or spiritual apathy? How seriously should we take it?

_____

_____

_____

24. (T) What does spiritual apathy look like in the Church today? How can we turn spiritual apathy into a love and passion for Christ (v. 20, Matthew 3:2, Luke 5:32, 1 John 1:9, James 5:16)?

_____

_____

_____

Verses 25-27

25. (E) What did Jesus praise the Father for regarding those who believe?

"That you have _____ these things from the _____ and _____ and _____ them to little _____."

26. How is this an example of an upside-down kingdom?

_____

_____

_____

27. Read 11:25 in the Contemporary English Version (CEV) of the Bible to help with your answers. Who are the "wise" ones who will refuse the message? (See question 15 for help.) Who are the "children" who will receive the message?

_____

_____

_____

_____

28. Read Psalm 19:7. How is a person made truly wise in the eyes of God?

_____

_____

_____

_____

29. (I) According to verse 27, how do people come to know the Father?

_____

_____

_____

_____

Verses 28-30

30. (I) How does verse 28 echo the first Beatitude?

_____

_____

_____

_____

_____

31. (I) The Jewish leaders burdened the people with their salvation by a works system, even adding 600+ of their own laws. How are verses 27-30 good news for the ordinary Jewish people (Ephesians 2:8-9)?

_____

_____

_____

_____

32. (I) Do these verses contradict Jesus's earlier statements to His disciples about the need for obedience and the inevitability of persecution? Why or why not?

_____

_____

_____

_____

33. (T) How are verses 28-30 good news for all?

_____

_____

_____

_____

34. (T) How are these verses good news for you personally? What heavy burden is causing your soul to be restless? Will you give it to the One who already carried the burden you were meant to carry to the cross with Him?

_____

_____

_____

_____

Day 3: Read Matthew 12:1-21

Verses 1-8

1. (E) Fill in the blanks for the following verses.

    Verse 1: "At that time Jesus went through the grainfields _____."

    Verse 2: "But when the _____ saw it, they said to him, 'Look, Your disciples are doing what is not lawful to do _____.'"

2. (E) Fill in the blanks of Jesus's response to the Pharisees.

    Verse 3: "He said to them, '_____ what David did when he was hungry, and those who were with him.'"

    Verse 5: "Or _____ in the Law how on the Sabbath the priests in the temple profane the Sabbath are guiltless?"

    Verse 6: "_____ , something greater than the temple is here."

3. (E) What did the Pharisees see Jesus's disciples doing when they were accused of breaking the Sabbath law?

    _____

    _____

    _____

    _____

    _____

4. (I) Read Deuteronomy 5:12-15 and 23:25. Did the disciples actually break God's command about the Sabbath? Why or why not?

    _____

    _____

    _____

    _____

    _____

5. (I) Jesus responds to the accusation with Scripture. He points them to the story of David and Ahimelech from 1 Samuel 21:1-6 to illustrate "I desire mercy not sacrifice." How do the actions of Ahimelech expose the hypocritical judging of the Pharisees? (Refer to the chart in Matthew 5, Day 5.)

    _____

    _____

    _____

6. (I) How does Ahimelech's example reveal the heart of God and the true intent of the ceremonial laws?

    _____

    _____

    _____

    _____

7. (I) Who is greater than David, the priests, and the temple?

    _____

    _____

    _____

    _____

8. (I) The temple was the Lord's holy dwelling place among His people and represented the heart of Jewish worship. How do you think the Pharisees felt about Jesus's statement in verse 6?

    _____

    _____

    _____

    _____

9. (I,T) How is Jesus the greater temple (John 1:14)? Why is this truth significant to believers more than 2,000 years later?

_____

_____

_____

10. (I) What is the claim Jesus is making about Himself when He says He is "Lord of the Sabbath"?

_____

_____

_____

Verses 9-13

11. (E) What was the intent of the Pharisees' question to Jesus in verse 10?

_____

_____

_____

12. (I) Paraphrase verses 11-12.

_____

_____

_____

13. (I) What attribute of Jesus do you see in these verses?

_____

_____

_____

14. (E,T) What was lawful to do on the Sabbath (v. 12)? How is this principle true for us today?

_____

_____

_____

15. (T) Jesus is saying that people are the most valuable gifts God has given us. How are you tempted to value tradition over relationships? How is the Church often guilty of valuing the institution over relationships? What can you do to start seeing people as God does— as a valued treasure?

_____

_____

_____

Verses 14-21

16. (E) What did the Pharisees conspire to do on the Sabbath?

_____

_____

_____

17. (I) What does this reveal about their hearts?

_____

_____

_____

18. (I) How is Christ the fulfillment of the prophecy from Isaiah 42:1-4?

_____

_____

_____

Day 4: Matthew 12:22-50

Verses 22-32

1. (E) What miracle does Jesus perform in verse 22?

    _____

    _____

    _____

2. (E) What was the response of the crowd after seeing this man healed?

    _____

    _____

    _____

3. (E) To whom do the Pharisees attribute Jesus's power?

    _____

    _____

    _____

4. (I) What do you think was the Pharisee's heart motive in discrediting Jesus in front of the crowd?

    _____

    _____

    _____

5. (I) Paraphrase verses 25-29.

    _____

    _____

    _____

6. (E) According to Jesus, what is the unpardonable sin?

    _____

    _____

    _____

7. (I) Read these verses again, and then explain what you think the unpardonable sin is. Keep in mind that the Pharisees knew who Jesus was but purposefully chose defiance.

    _____

    _____

    _____

8. (T) How are people today still guilty of the unpardonable sin? (Psalm 19:1) What does the text say the fate is for those who commit this sin (v. 32, John 3:36)?

    _____

    _____

    _____

Verses 33-37

9. (I) According to these verses, how does a person's speech reveal what is in their heart?

    _____

    _____

    _____

10. (E) According to these verses, what does the Pharisees' speech reveal about them?

    _____

    _____

    _____

11. (E,T) According to verse 36, who will give an account for their words? How does this encourage you? Warn you?

_____

_____

_____

_____

Verses 38-42

12. (I) What kind of sign did the Pharisees want (Mark 8:11)? What do you think that means?

_____

_____

_____

_____

13. (E) According to Jesus, who seeks a sign (v. 39)?

_____

_____

_____

_____

14. (E) What did Jesus say will be the ultimate sign given to the Pharisees (v. 39)?

"but no sign will be given to it except the _____."

15. (I) Verse 40 tells us exactly what that sign is. What future event is Jesus referencing (1 Corinthians 15:4)?

_____

_____

_____

16. (I) Jesus gives two accounts—the people of Ninevah and the Queen of Sheba—as a testimony to the Pharisees' judgment and condemnation. Match the people group with the correct description. (See Jonah 1-4 and 1 Kings 10:1-13 for further reading.)

People of Ninevah/Queen of Sheba

Gentiles
God's Covenant people
Idol Worshipers
Jews

The scribes, Pharisees, religious leaders

repented/honored
unbelief
did not have the law
had the law

17. (I) Who is the greater Jonah and Solomon? In what ways?

_____

_____

_____

18. (T) Does your faith require extrabiblical experiences or signs? What could be problematic about this approach?

_____

_____

_____

Verses 43-45

19. (I) Match each element from the parable to what it represents.

Unclean spirit

Religious Leaders

Waterless places

works salvation/fruitlessness

Rest

immorality/vile character

House

Salvation in Christ

Evil generation

The Heart

20. (I) Does this parable illustrate someone who is getting wiser or more foolish and sinful? How do you know?

_____

_____

_____

_____

21. (I) Why do you think Matthew places this parable at this place in the narrative?

_____

_____

_____

_____

Verses 46-50

22. (E) What does verse 50 tell us is the evidence of being a member of God's family?

_____

_____

_____

_____

23. (T) What does doing God's will look like in your life ?

_____

_____

_____

_____

_____

_____

Day 5: Read Matthew 13

Verses 1-9, 18-23

1. (E) Look up the word *parable* in a dictionary and write a definition for it.

    _____

    _____

2. (I) Why are stories useful and powerful tools?

    _____

    _____

3. (I) One reason Jesus speaks in hard-to-understand parables is to veil the truth from unbelievers. How is this an example of God's mercy (Luke 12:47-48, Romans 2:5-8, Hebrews 10:26-29)?

    _____

    _____

4. (E) Draw a line matching each element from the story to what it represents.

Sower	The Word/Gospel message
Seed	Hearers and responses to the message
Soil	The Lord and all those who preach the Gospel
Hard soil	Superficial heart – those with a superficial root
Rocky soil	Divided heart – those who love the world
Thorny soil	Hard heart – those who reject Christ
Good soil	Converted heart – those who are genuinely saved
Birds	Persecution
Thorns	Fruit of belief
Crop	Evil One

5. (T) What are some "thorns" in your life? What can you do practically to keep them from chocking your faith?

_____

_____

_____

6. (E) According to verses 8 and 23, what is the distinguishing mark of the "good soil"?

_____

_____

_____

7. (I,T) How can these verses be an encouragement for the sower? How can they be an encouragement for you personally?

_____

_____

_____

Verses 10-17

8. (I) Summarize Jesus's response in verses 11-13 to the disciples' question from verse 10.

_____

_____

_____

9. (I) In verse 11, who is the "you" Jesus refers to? Who is "them"?

"And He answered them, To you it has been given to know the secrets of the kingdom of heaven, but to them it has not been given."

_____

_____

10. (I) How are these verses a fulfillment of Isaiah 6:9-10? What does the Isaiah passage teach us about God? About mankind?

_____

_____

_____

11. (E) How are the disciples blessed (vv. 16-17)?

_____

_____

_____

Verses 24-30, 36-43

12. (I) Draw a line matching each element from the story to what it represents.

Sower	Jesus
Field	Believers; righteous ones
Wheat	Satan
Weeds	World
Enemy	Unbelievers; lawless ones
Harvest	Angels
Reapers	End of age

13. (I) Verse 25 in the New English Translation (NET) of the Bible says, "while everyone was sleeping." How does the phrase "while everyone was sleeping" help you understand how Satan opposes Christ's work?

_____

_____

_____

_____

14. (I) After reading the first two parables, what seems to be the primary calling of God's children (sowing the seed or pulling the weeds)?

_____

_____

_____

Verses 31-35

15. (E) Fill in the blanks.

It is the _____ of all seeds, but when it has _____ it is _____ than all the garden plants and becomes a tree, so that the birds of the air come and make nests in its branches" (vv. 31-32).

"The kingdom of heaven is like leaven that a woman took and hid in the three measures of flour, till it was _____ leavened" (v. 34).

16. (I) How do these parables relate to Kingdom expansion and growth?

_____

_____

_____

17. (T) How does the history of the Church prove these parables?

_____

_____

_____

18. (I) How does Psalm 78:2 find fulfillment in Christ?

_____

_____

_____

Verses 44-46

19. (E) What two things represent the kingdom of heaven in these verses?

_____

_____

_____

20. (E) What did the man and the merchant do upon finding their treasure?

_____

_____

_____

21. (I) What spiritual truth is Jesus communicating in these verses?

_____

_____

_____

22. (T) How can you be more like the man and the merchant in these parables? What can you willingly give up to completely follow Christ?

_____

_____

_____

Verses 47-50

23. (I) How is this parable similar to the wheat and weeds parable?

_____

_____

_____

24. (I) What eternal truths are both parables communicating?

_____

_____

_____

Verses 51-52

25. (I) Who are the "scribes who have been trained up for the kingdom of heaven" (v. 36)? (E) What does a "scribe who has been trained for the kingdom of heaven" do?

_____

_____

_____

26. (I) What old (think law and prophets) and new treasures do these scribes possess?

_____

_____

_____

27. (I) How are these scribes different from the scribes in Jesus's audience?

_____

_____

_____

28. (I) Why would it be important for Jesus to ask them if they understood "all these things"? (Think about who some of the authors of the New Testament are.)

_____

_____

_____

29. (T) What about you? Have you understood "all these things"? What do you need to know in order to be able to share the message of the Kingdom with others?

_____

_____

_____

_____

Verses 53-58

30. (I) Paraphrase the reaction of the people in Jesus's hometown.

_____

_____

_____

_____

31. (E,I) What was Jesus's response to their unbelief? How is this an act of both judgment and mercy?

_____

_____

_____

_____

32. (T) How can familiarity of a brother or sister in Christ hinder us from recognizing God's presence in their ministry? What can we do to ensure we honor those God has sent to do "mighty works"?

_____

_____

_____

_____

Day 6: Commit what you learned to prayer. Reread Matthew 11-13.

Adoration:

"God, you are......."

Pray the attributes of God we studied this week back to God.

Confession:

"Lord, I confess....."

In light of the above and what we studied this week, what did you learn about yourself?

Thanksgiving:

"Thank you......."

What from this week's passage made your heart overflow with thanksgiving?

Supplication:

"I lift up......"

After reading this week's passage, what petitions do you need to ask from God?

Global: _____

Local: _____

Personal: _____

MATTHEW 14-15

His Power Shines in Our Weakness

AIM: His power shines in our weakness.

Scripture to Memorize:

And I tell you, you are Peter, and on this rock I will build my church, and the gates of hell shall not prevail against it.

—Matt. 16:18

Attribute of God: Infinite

God is unlimited. He has no limits in His person, His knowledge, or His power. He is Omniscient, Omnipotent, and Omnipresent. He has always existed and always will with no beginning and no end. He is not limited by space or time. He is infinitely above and beyond our ability to fully comprehend all He is. God is completely separate, independent, and far greater than His creation. There is no way to measure God.

Doctrine: The Church

The Church is the assembly of born-again people who have been redeemed by Jesus's sacrifice on the cross. It is God's dwelling place on Earth. It is not a building or a denomination, but a living organism of people dedicated to serving Christ, His Kingdom, and His people. Christ is the head, the architect, the designer, the builder, and the cornerstone of the Church. The cornerstone is the point that holds the foundation together. The foundation is built by the apostles and prophets. It was through the apostles and prophets God spoke to His people and delivered His Word. The foundation of the Church is the Word of God. The Word of God is imperishable, and nothing can stop or defeat Christ's Church, nor can any powers of hell or evil stop its growth. The Church is unstoppable because the Holy Spirit is unstoppable.

A person's decision to come to faith in Christ is an individual decision, however, the Christian life was never intended to be in isolation. Biblical metaphors for a church are always plural, never singular, such as body, flock, household, and holy nation. The Church will not be finished until Christ's return. The household of Christ walks according to the power of the Holy Spirit and shines as a light to the world for God's glory. God loves His Church and has given her as a bride to God's Son, Jesus. He will return one day to collect His bride.

There is a visible and also invisible reality to the Church. In the Old Testament, the entire nation of Israel composed of God's people, however, only those within Israel who had faith would be saved for eternity. The same is true for the New Testament Church. The visible church can include those whose faith is not genuine. The invisible Church is only known to God. He will separate the true believers from the false professors at the right time. Until then, we are to meet together, pray together, fellowship together, and faithfully teach and preach God's Word. We will spend all eternity worshipping with other redeemed saints, the great reality and privilege is that God has allowed us to start right now.

Day 1: Read Matthew 14-15

1. In two to three sentences, summarize what happens in these chapters.

   Chapter 14

   _____

   _____

   _____

   Chapter 15

   _____

   _____

   _____

2. Reflect on how those who heard and saw Jesus did not reject Him for lack of evidence but in spite of overwhelming evidence. Why do you think that is?

   _____

   _____

   _____

Day 2: Read Matthew 14:1-21

Verses 1-12

1. (E) Who did Herod believe Jesus was? Why did he think that?

_____

_____

_____

2. (E) Why did Herod imprison John?

_____

_____

_____

3. (E) Read Leviticus 18:16 and note what it says.

_____

_____

_____

4. (T) Describe a time you have been persecuted for speaking the truth.

_____

_____

_____

5. (I) Based on their motives and actions, describe the characters of Herod and Herodias.

_____

_____

_____

6. (I) Review the chart from Matthew 5, Day 5 and notice that an earthly kingdom is characterized by anger, lust, low view of marriage, flippant with oaths, revenge, and hate. Write a verse number (1–12) next to the character trait where it is best demonstrated in this section. One has been done for you.

Anger   – v. 3

Lust   _____

Low view of marriage   _____

Flippant with oaths   _____

Revenge   _____

Hate   _____

7. (T) Herod and Herodias' sin starts in the heart with anger and ends with the outward act of murder. How is this progression of sin living out Jesus's main point in Matthew 5:21–28? How does this progression of sin warn you personally?

_____

_____

_____

8. (I) What stands out to you in the response of John the Baptist's disciples?

_____

_____

_____

_____

Verses 13–14

9. (E) Read verse 13 and answer the following questions about Jesus.

What did he hear?

_____

_____

What did he do?

_____

_____

Where did he go?

_____

_____

10. (I) What do these verses show us about the heart of Jesus?

_____

_____

_____

11. (E) Fill in the blanks from verse 14.

"When he went ashore he saw a great crowd, and he had _____ on them and healed their sick."

12. (T) What does this teach us about turning our own inward sorrow into outward acts of compassion for others?

_____

_____

_____

Verses 15-21

13. (E) What is the disciples' practical concern in verses 15-17? How did Jesus respond in verse 16?

_____

_____

_____

14. (I) Another word for "desolate" is *desert* or *wilderness*. Jesus is providing the Jewish people bread and meat in the wilderness. Read Exodus 16. Who else did this? What claim is Jesus making about Himself through this miracle?

_____

_____

_____

15. (I) What does this miracle say about Jesus's authority?

_____

_____

_____

_____

16. (E) Fill in the blanks from verse 20.

"And they _____ ate and were _____."

17. (I) What spiritual truth is being taught through Jesus's feeding of the 5,000 (John 6:35, 10:10)?

_____

_____

_____

_____

18. (T) When has God provided a banquet for you in the "wilderness"?

_____

_____

_____

19. (I) Match the physical items with its symbolic representation.

Bread   Salvation for the Gentiles

12 baskets   Jews/12 tribes of Israel

Broken pieces left over   Jesus/salvation

20. (T) What lesson(s) did Jesus want His disciples to learn? What lesson(s) can you learn from these verses?

_____

_____

_____

_____

Day 3: Read Matthew 14:22-36

Verses 22-33

1. (E,I) What did Jesus do on the mountain in verse 23? What does this reveal about Jesus?

_____

_____

_____

_____

2. (I) Why do you think Jesus sent the disciples ahead of Him in the boat?

_____

_____

_____

_____

_____

3. (E,I) The disciples would have been rowing for somewhere between six and eight hours. Why do you think Jesus allowed His followers to struggle that long (2 Corinthians 12:9-10 and the aim)?

    _____

    _____

    _____

    _____

4. (I) Verse 25 says Jesus walked on the sea. Think back to 8:23-27. What does Jesus have authority over?

    _____

    _____

    _____

    _____

5. (E) In verse 26, what was the disciples' response to seeing Jesus walk on the sea?

    _____

    _____

    _____

    _____

6. (E) Fill in the blank with the response of Jesus.

    "But immediately Jesus spoke to them, saying, 'Take heart; _____. Do not be afraid.'"

7. The Amplified Bible, Classic Edition (AMPC) has a closer, more literal translation of these words. Fill in the blanks from this version.

    "But instantly He spoke to them, saying, Take courage! _____! Stop being afraid."

8. (I) What is significant about those words? Read the following verses and note what you read. What claim is Jesus making about Himself?

Genesis 15:1

_____

_____

Genesis 46:3

_____

_____

Exodus 3:1-14

_____

_____

Isaiah 41:4

_____

_____

Isaiah 41:13

_____

_____

Isaiah 43:1-4

_____

_____

9. (E) What did Peter ask and do in verses 28-29? What does that reveal about Peter?

_____

_____

_____

10. (E) Where was Peter's focus in verse 30?

    "But when he _____ the _____."

11. (E,T) In verse 30, what happened when he took his focus off Jesus and on the wind? What spiritual truth can we learn from this?

    _____

    _____

    _____

12. (T) What are some fears or circumstances that cause you to take your focus off of Christ? What are some practical steps you can take this week to submit those fears to the One who says to you, "I AM, do not be afraid."

    _____

    _____

    _____

13. (E) What does Peter cry out in verse 30?

    _____

    _____

    _____

    _____

14. (E,T) How quickly does Jesus respond when Peter cries out for help? How does this truth encourage you?

    _____

    _____

    _____

    _____

15. (I) Do you believe Jesus is rebuking Peter in verse 31? Why or why not?

_____

_____

_____

16. (E) What happened when Jesus got into the boat?

_____

_____

_____

17. (E) What was the response of the disciples?

_____

_____

_____

18. (I) Reread Matthew 8:27. Compare the response of the disciples in this verse with their response in verse 33. What change do you see?

_____

_____

_____

_____

19. (I) In light of the above question, what do you think Jesus's intentions are in 14:15-33?

_____

_____

_____

_____

20. (T) What circumstances in your life has God used to reveal His power and presence and to strengthen your faith?

_____

_____

_____

Verses 34-36

21. (E) Compare the accounts of Jesus in His hometown (13:53-58) and the accounts of Jesus in Gennesaret. How do these illustrate His parable of the soils in chapter 13?

_____

_____

_____

Day 4: Read Matthew 15:1-20

Verses 1-9

1. (E) Fill in the blanks. What concern did the Pharisees and scribes have in these verses?

   "Why do your disciples break the _____ of the _____ ?"

2. (E) What concern did Jesus have? Fill in the blanks.

   "Why do you break the _____ of _____ for the sake of _____ ?"

3. (I) Jesus uses a specific commandment to give proof of their corruption of the law. Read Mark 7:11-13. How did the Pharisees reject the commandment of God in order to keep their own tradition?

_____

_____

_____

4. (T) How do we tend to value manmade religious tradition over divine truth?

_____

_____

_____

_____

5. (E,I) Look up the word _hypocrite_ in the dictionary. Write a definition of it below that best fits the way it is used in verse 7.

_____

_____

_____

_____

6. (I) Explain how Jesus turned an external matter of washing hands into an internal matter of the heart? How does Jesus's rebuke of the Pharisees in these verses reemphasize His previous rebuke regarding external and internal obedience? (Read the following verses to help with your answer: 1 Samuel 15:22, 16:7, Hosea 6:6, Matthew 9:13).

_____

_____

_____

_____

7. (T) In what ways do you ignore or excuse hypocrisy in yourself?

_____

_____

_____

_____

Verses 10-20

8. (I) Paraphrase verses 11, 18, and 19. What is the main principle Jesus teaches the crowd? How does it relate to Matthew 12:33-34?

_____

_____

_____

_____

9. (T) Jesus calls the Pharisees "blind guides" in verse 14. How is Christ's parable about the blind leading the blind just as relevant today? What are some examples?

_____

_____

_____

_____

10. (I) What actually defiles a person in God's sight? (v.18)

_____

_____

_____

_____

11. (E) List the sinful actions that Jesus says come out of an unclean heart in verse 19. Why do you think Jesus does not give an account of all the good things that comes out of the heart (Jeremiah 17:9)?

_____

_____

_____

_____

12. (I) How does this verse (15:19) relate to the Sermon on the Mount?

_____

_____

_____

13. (T) What external activities do people perform as a means to be right with God? What is the only way to be made right with God (Psalm 51:10, Ezekiel 36:26, Matthew 5:8, 2 Corinthians 5:17, John 3:16)?

_____

_____

_____

Day 5: Matthew 15:21-39

Verses 21-28

1. (E) Fill in the blanks from verse 22.

   "And behold, a _____ from that region came out and was crying, 'Have mercy on me, O _____. My daughter is severely oppressed by a demon.'"

2. (E,I) What term does the Canaanite woman use for Jesus three times (vv. 22, 25, 27)? What does that reveal about the woman?

_____

_____

_____

3. What are the disciples concerned with in verse 23?

_____

_____

_____

4. (I) Think back to 14:13-21. How do the broken pieces left over from verse 20 help us better understand what is being communicated in verse 27?

_____

_____

_____

_____

5. (I) How is this woman embodying the Beatitudes?

_____

_____

_____

_____

6. (I) How did Jesus describe this Gentile woman's faith in verse 28? Who else had similar faith (8:5-13)?

_____

_____

_____

_____

7. (T) The Canaanite (Gentile) woman was essentially asking Jesus if there was room at His table (salvation) for her. What was Jesus's answer to the woman (v. 28)? Who is Jesus calling you to invite and share a meal with at your table in the presence of the Lord?

_____

_____

_____

_____

8. (I) Jesus took His disciples outside the boundaries of Israel at this time. What lesson did the disciples need to learn about Gentiles and salvation?

_____

_____

_____

_____

Verses 29-31

9. (E) List all the ways Jesus compassionately met the needs of the crowd in this section.

_____

_____

_____

_____

10. (I) Match the people group on the left with the spiritual truth on the right.

Israelites (15:10-20)   blind seeing, lame walking, mute speaking, glorifying the God of Israel

Gentiles (15:29-31)   blind leading the blind, spiritually crippled, mute in glorying God

Verses 32-39

11. (E,I) What practical concern is in verse 33? How is the faith of the disciples in contrast to the woman's from the previous section (vv. 21-28)?

_____

_____

_____

_____

_____

12. (I) How is this section similar to 14:13-21? How is it different? (Keep in mind that Jesus is in a Gentile region.)

_____

_____

_____

13. (I) Match the physical items with its symbolic representation.

Bread   Salvation for the Gentiles

Seven baskets   Completion

Broken pieces left over   Jesus/salvation

14. (I,T) How might the feeding of the 4,000 symbolize completion (Matthew 16:18, Galatians 3:28, Ephesians 2:19-20)? How does this truth impact you personally?

_____

_____

_____

15. (I) How might this repeated miracle have benefited the disciples?

_____

_____

_____

_____

16. (T) How does the truth only Jesus can satisfy help with your need today?

_____

_____

_____

_____

17. (E) How does Jesus end His ministry in Galilee (Matthew 14:13-21)? How does He end His ministry in the Gentile regions (Matthew 15:32-29)? What does that reveal about Jesus and His mission?

_____

_____

_____

_____

18. (I) Match the left side to the correct descriptions on the right.

	Rejected Jesus
The Jews	Received Jesus
	Vain worship
The Gentiles	Glorified God
	Sent to first
	Sent to after

Day 6: Commit what you learned to prayer. Reread Matthew 14-15.

Adoration:

"God, you are...."

Pray the attributes of God we studied this week back to God.

Confession:

"Lord, I confess...."

In light of the above and what we studied this week, what did you learn about yourself?

Thanksgiving:

"Thank you...."

What from this week's passage made your heart overflow with thanksgiving?

Supplication:

"I lift up…."

After reading this week's passage, what petitions do you need to ask of God?

Global: _____

Local: _____

Personal: _____

MATTHEW 16-17

Jesus Is the Better Moses and Elijah

AIM: Jesus is the better Moses and Elijah.

Scripture to Memorize:

But who do you say that I am?? Simon Peter replied, "You are the Christ, the Son of the living God."

–Matt. 16:15-16

Attribute of God: Glory

God's glory is the total of all His attributes – His power, mercy, grace, judgment, holiness, love, righteousness, and every other attribute. It defines the very essence of God's being and the very presence of God among His people. In the Old Testament, His glory was manifested in a cloud or what scholars call the Shekinah glory, the dwelling presence of God with His people. In the New Testament, the glory of God is fully revealed in His Son, Jesus Christ. John 1:14 says, "The Word became flesh and dwelt among us, and we have seen His glory, glory as the of the only Son from the Father, full of grace and truth." Jesus is the true glory of God.

Doctrine: Suffering

When Adam and Eve disobeyed God in the garden, the result was sin. Sin affected every aspect of life and opened the door of suffering to all of creation. Even though suffering is the result of sin in the world, not all suffering is directly related to personal sin. There are many sources such as our own sin, the sins of others, and the natural consequences of living in a fallen world. Suffering can be spiritual, physical, mental, or emotional and affects all aspects of human relationships. Most of us probably do not rejoice in the pain and affliction when it comes our way, but we can rejoice knowing it does not happen outside of God's sovereign control. God is good and everything He does is good. He allows suffering and can use it for His glory and our good. It is not for nothing. It is through suffering God draws us near, grows our faith and strengthens us, prepares us to minister to others, and calls the wicked to repentance. It makes us long for eternity where there will be no more sorrow, pain, weeping, or sin, but the way to this glory is through suffering. God uses our momentary affliction to prepare believers for eternal glory.

Jesus is the perfect example as the Suffering Servant. He suffered in a way we can never fully comprehend. He humbled Himself to the point of death on the cross. He took the ultimate suffering of His people for His people. And is now exalted and seated at the right hand of the Father. Jesus allowed himself to be sorrowful during these times, but He also kept focus on the final outcome. Jesus did not look at suffering as something He needed to just "get through." He kept His eyes on God and His plans and purposes. The Church participates in Christ's suffering but knowing we belong to Him we can see suffering as a gift. And because we suffer with Him, we will also be raised with Him. We can endure temporary adversity because of the eternal hope we have in Christ. For those who do not know Christ and Him crucified will suffer for all eternity. There will be no comfort, rest, or relief for them. Suffering will never end. The only thing that will ultimately relive suffering is the Gospel so we must continue to preach the good news.

Day 1: Read Matthew 16-17

1. In two to three sentences, summarize what happens in these chapters.

Chapter 16

_____

_____

_____

Chapter 17

_____

_____

_____

_____

2. What can you do to honor Christ for who He is and what He has done?

   _____

   _____

   _____

Day 2: Read Matthew 16:1-12

Verses 1-4

1. (E) Fill in the blanks from verse 1.

   "And the _____ and _____ came, and to
   _____ him they asked him to show them a _____
   from _____."

2. (E) *Tested* can also be translated "tempted." Who else tempted Jesus (Matthew 4)?

   _____

   _____

   _____

3. (E) What "signs of the times" (signs and wonders) had Jesus already been doing (Matthew 4:23-25, 11:5, 15:29-31)?

   _____

   _____

   _____

4. (I) Review your notes on Matthew 12:38-42. Paraphrase Jesus's response to the religious leaders in verse 4. Why is this sign sufficient?

   _____

   _____

   _____

Verses 5-12

5. (E) What physical concern did the disciples have in these verses? What miracle just happened that Jesus needed to remind the disciples of?

    _____

    _____

    _____

6. (T) How is your faith strengthened by remembering the past faithfulness of God?

    _____

    _____

    _____

    _____

7. (E) What did Jesus tell them they needed to be concerned with in verse 12?

    "Then they understood that he did not tell them to beware of the _____ of bread, but of the _____ of the Pharisees and Sadducees."

8. (T) How can we often miss the spiritual meaning like the disciples did?

    _____

    _____

    _____

    _____

9. (I) Why would leaven be a good comparison for the false teaching of the Pharisees? Read the following verses and note what they say.

    Galatians 5:9

    _____

    _____

1 Corinthians 5:6-7

_____

_____

1 Corinthians 15:33

_____

_____

10. (T) Is the "leaven" of the Pharisees and Sadducees something the modern-day church needs to be concerned with? Why or why not?

_____

_____

_____

11. (T) What sin in your life needs to be dealt with so it does not grow and spread?

_____

_____

_____

Day 3: Matthew 16:13-23

Verses 13-16

1. (E,I) What two questions did Jesus ask? What do you notice about the progression between these two questions? Why is the progression important?

_____

_____

_____

_____

2. (E) How did the disciples answer the first question?

_____

_____

_____

3. (T) How do people answer that question today?

_____

_____

_____

4. (E) How did Peter answer the second question? (Note: This is the first time in Matthew's Gospel that someone refers to Jesus as "Christ.")

_____

_____

_____

5. (E) Read the following verses and take note of what they say.

    Deuteronomy 5:26

_____

_____

    Joshua 3:10

_____

_____

    1 Samuel 17:26

_____

_____

2 Kings 19:4

_____

_____

Daniel 6:26

_____

_____

Hosea 1:10

_____

_____

6. (I) Match the following descriptions with the title.

Christ   God of the OT/fulfillment of OT promises

Son of   Anointed/Chosen One

Living God   Characteristics/nature of

7. (I) Why is Jesus's second question the most critical question in life? How do you answer this question?

_____

_____

_____

Verses 17-20

8. (E,T) Based on verse 17, who should receive credit for someone understanding spiritual truth (Ephesians 2:8-9)? How does this truth impact you today?

_____

_____

_____

9. (I) Read Genesis 17. God gives Abram a new name, new people, and a promise. What similarities do you see in 16:17-20? How is 16:17-20 a continuation of Genesis 17?

_____

_____

_____

10. (I) Read Isaiah 51:1-2. How do these verses bridge the thought between Genesis 17 and Matthew 16:17-20?

_____

_____

_____

11. (E) According to verse 18, who is the architect of Christ's Church? Who is the builder? The owner?

_____

_____

_____

12. (I) What is the Church? (Read the doctrine to help with your answer.)

_____

_____

_____

13. (E,T) What is significant about the way Jesus describes His Church in verse 18? How does this truth encourage you?

_____

_____

_____

14. (I) Keys represent the Gospel and the opening of the Kingdom for all those who believe. Verse 19 expresses this power of the Gospel. Paraphrase verse 19.

_____

_____

_____

15. (T) How is Jesus at work building His Church today?

_____

_____

_____

16. (T) How has the power of the Gospel impacted your life?

_____

_____

_____

17. (I) Why do you think Jesus gave this specific charge in verse 20 to the disciples(John 7:6)?

_____

_____

_____

Verses 21-23

18. (E) What did Jesus begin to reveal to the disciples in verse 21?

_____

_____

_____

_____

19. (E) What was Peter's response to this revelation (v. 22)?

_____

_____

_____

20. (I) Paraphrase verse 23.

_____

_____

_____

21. (I,T) Why do you think Jesus rebuked Peter so harshly in verse 23? (Look at the second part of verse 23.) What do you learn from this?

_____

_____

_____

22. (E) Who else tried to tempt Jesus to skip the cross and suffering and go straight to glory (Matthew 4)?

_____

_____

_____

23. (T) Jesus's praise for Peter in verse 17 quickly switched to His rebuke in verse 23. In what ways can you relate to this?

_____

_____

_____

_____

24. (T) What does shifting your focus from the things of mankind to the things of God look like in your life? How does suffering fit into the things of God?

_____

_____

_____

_____

Day 4: Matthew 16:24-17:21

Verses 24-28

1. (I) How does verse 24 continue the thought from verse 23?

_____

_____

_____

_____

2. (I) Explain how God's Kingdom in these verses is an example of an upside-down kingdom.

_____

_____

_____

_____

3. (T) What does self-denial look like in your life?

_____

_____

_____

_____

4. (T) In what ways have you had to "take up your cross" and encounter hardship because you follow Jesus? Do you think it is worth it? Why or why not?

_____

_____

_____

_____

5. (T) Verses 27-28 have been interpreted in various ways. What warning or encouragement should we take from them regardless?

_____

_____

_____

_____

Verses 17:1-8

6. (I) Read Exodus 24:1-18 and 34:29 and compare them with Matthew 17:1-2. What are some similarities? What are some differences?

_____

_____

_____

_____

7. (I) Look up the word _transfiguration_ in the dictionary. Write a definition of it below that best fits the way it is used in the passage.

_____

_____

_____

_____

8. (E) What two features of change are mentioned in verse 2?

    _____

    _____

    _____

    _____

9. (E,I) Who also appeared on the mountain in verses 3-4? What is the significance of their appearing and speaking with Jesus (Exodus 34:29, Deuteronomy 18:15, 1 Kings 19:8-9, Matthew 5:17)?

    _____

    _____

    _____

    _____

10. (E) What was Peter's suggestion and immediate response to the scene (v. 4)? Who interrupted Peter in verse 5, and what did He say? (Read Deuteronomy 18:15, Matthew 3:17, and Acts 3:22-26 for extra understanding of the words.)

    _____

    _____

    _____

    _____

11. (E,I) What were the reactions of the disciples after the voice spoke? Why does this seem to be the appropriate response for those who have been in the presence of God?

    _____

    _____

    _____

    _____

12. (I) What did Jesus do in verses 7–8? What does this reveal about Jesus?

_____

_____

_____

13. (I) Peter reflects on the Transfiguration years later in 2 Peter 1:17-21. What does Peter mention is even more valuable than the firsthand experience of witnessing the Transfiguration?

_____

_____

_____

14. (T) God continues to instruct us even today to "listen to Him" through His revealed Word. What does this look like in your life today?

_____

_____

_____

Verses 9-13

15. (E) Fill in the blanks from verse 9.

"Tell _____ the vision, until the Son of Man is _____."

16. (E,I) What event is Jesus referring to in verse 9 (1 Peter 1:3)? Why do you think He gives the instructions to the disciples to wait until this certain time?

_____

_____

_____

_____

17. (I) Read Malachi 4:5. What do you think the disciples were confused about?

_____

_____

_____

18. (E) Who was the "Elijah" these verses are referring to? What happened to him (Matthew 14:1-12)?

_____

_____

_____

19. (E,I) At the end of verse 12, what does Jesus remind the disciples will also happen to Him? Why do you think He continues to mention this?

_____

_____

_____

Verses 14-21

20. (E) What was the son's affliction, and what did it cause him to do according to verse 15?

_____

_____

_____

21. (T) What are some modern-day, self-destructive behaviors?

_____

_____

_____

22. (E) Who did the man take his son to for healing and what was the result (v. 16)?

_____

_____

_____

23. (I) What does verse 18 reveal about Jesus? (Think back to Matthew 8:28-32).

_____

_____

_____

24. (E) What was the disciples' concern in verse 19 (v. 16)? (Review Matthew 10:6-8.)

_____

_____

_____

25. (I) Fill in the blanks with Jesus's response in verse 20.

"Because of your _____."

26. (E) What other insight does Mark 9:29 give us? (Also, read verse 21 in the KJV)

_____

_____

_____

27. (I) Explain the connection between faith and prayer.

_____

_____

_____

28. (T) What is your prayer life like? How does your prayer life reveal your belief and trust in God?

_____

_____

_____

29. (I) What is the difference between "little faith" that Jesus rebukes and "small faith" that He blesses?

_____

_____

_____

30. (I) What is Jesus teaching about faith? Circle one.

The size of our faith influences its power.

The object of our faith influences its power, regardless of its size.

31. (T) What mountains (situations or sins) do you feel are too big even for the Lord to move? How can God use these mountains to grow your faith?

_____

_____

_____

32. (T) How are the lessons taught in these first few verses–listen to Him (Jesus) and pray–still lessons for the Church today?

_____

_____

_____

_____

Day 5: Matthew 17:22-27

Verses 22-23

1. (E,I) What made the disciples "greatly distressed"–"exceedingly sorrowful" in the New King James Version (NKJV)? How does this show they lacked a full understanding of Jesus's words and purpose?

_____

_____

_____

2. (T) How have you experienced great grief or sorrow because you did not understand God's greater plan?

_____

_____

_____

3. (I) What divine attribute do these verses reveal about Jesus?

_____

_____

_____

Verses 24-27

4. (E) What concern did the tax collectors have in verse 24? (Read this verse in the NIV to understand what kind of tax is being collected.)

_____

_____

_____

_____

5. (I) Read Exodus 30:11-16. What was the intent of this tax?

_____

_____

_____

6. (E) According to Jesus in verses 25-26, was the son of the temple king required or not required to pay the tax?

_____

_____

_____

7. (I) Who is the "king of the temple" in this parable? Who then is the "son of the king of the temple" in this parable?

_____

_____

_____

8. (I) Why did Jesus tell Peter to catch a fish and open its mouth to find the shekel instead of just giving him one? What truths do you think Jesus wanted to teach through this miracle?

_____

_____

_____

9. (E,T) Does Jesus end up paying the temple tax or not? What reason does He give? What lesson can you learn from this?

_____

_____

_____

10. (I) How will Jesus ultimately pay for the temple tax that is to be an atonement for the people's lives (Matthew 27:32-44)?

_____

_____

_____

Day 6: Commit what you learned to prayer. Reread Matthew 16-17.

Adoration:

"God, you are…."

Pray the attributes of God we studied this week back to God.

Confession:

"Lord, I confess…."

In light of the above and what we studied this week, what did you learn about yourself?

Thanksgiving:

"Thank you…."

What from this week's passage made your heart overflow with thanksgiving?

Supplication:

"I lift up…."

After reading this week's passage, what petitions do you need to ask from God?

Global: _____

Local: _____

Personal: _____

MATTHEW 18-20

Christ and His Kingdom Exceed Everything This Life Has to Offer

AIM: Christ and His Kingdom exceed everything this life has to offer.

Scripture to Memorize:

But many who are first will be last, and the last first.

–Matt. 19:30

Attribute of God: Jealous

The jealousy used to describe God is different than how it is used to describe the sin of jealousy. To say God is jealous is to say all glory belongs to Him and Him alone. He will not share it with another. This is not because He feels insecure, but because He loves His people and does not want them devoted to themselves and worship lesser things.

Doctrine: Grace

Grace is one of the prominent themes in all Scripture. The word grace translated means "favor," "blessing," or "kindness." It is the essence of God's character that leads to giving us what we do not deserve. It is the only way anyone can enter into a relationship with God. Ephesians 2:8 says, "For by grace you have been saved through faith. And this is not your own doing; it is the gift of God." There is nothing anyone can do to earn God's favor, and nothing is owed in return. God rejected the many who thought they could earn their own salvation and instead blessed those who came to Him in humble submission and their awareness of their need of a Savior. The saying "grace upon grace" is because God's grace is abundant. It is fully manifested in Jesus Christ and those who trust in Christ are showered with His abundant grace. We cannot meet God's divine standards and deserve punishment. But, Christ came, obeyed every law perfectly, and rescues fallen humanity from our deserved punishment. He exchanged His righteousness for our sin. Even though grace is a gift, it did not come without a cost. It came at great cost to Jesus Christ, who died in our place.

When we rightly view our sinfulness and become mindful that we cannot do anything - even breathe - apart from God's grace, we live differently. We understand everything in our life is a gift from God. It creates a sense of thankfulness and purpose from the biggest to even the smallest and mundane aspects of our life. As recipients of God's grace, we desire to extend grace to others. We want to serve and be good stewards of the gifts God has given us. Grace inspired one of the greatest hymns ever written, *Amazing Grace*. John Newton understood that it was only by God's grace alone we wake up each morning, God's grace that is with us and leads us in each and every trial and tribulation, it is God's grace that is greater than all our sin, and it will be by God's grace that will lead us to eternity with Him. His grace will be ours to enjoy forever.

Day 1: Read Matthew 18-20

1.   In two to three sentences, summarize what happens in these chapters.

Chapter 18

_____

_____

_____

Chapter 19

_____

_____

_____

Chapter 20

_____

_____

_____

2. Chapter 18 begins the fourth of five discourses. Summarize each discourse thus far (Matthew 5-7, 10, 13, 18).

    _____

    _____

    _____

    _____

Day 2: Read Matthew 18

Verses 1-4

1. (E) What was the question the disciples asked Jesus?

    _____

    _____

    _____

    _____

2. (I) The first three words in verse 1—"at this time"—connect us to the previous chapter. How might the events at the end of chapter 17 have influenced this particular question from the disciples?

    _____

    _____

    _____

    _____

3. (E) Fill in the blanks with Jesus's response in verse 3-4.

    "Truly, I say to you, unless you _____ and become _____ , you will _____ the kingdom of heaven. Whoever _____ himself like this child is the greatest in the kingdom of heaven."

4. (I) How does Jesus's response (v. 3) differ from the actual question the disciples asked (v. 1)?

_____

_____

_____

5. (I) Circle the description that best fits the "humble" that Jesus is referring to in verse 4.

Innocent and pure

cute and cuddly

dependent and helpless

6. (I) How is this principle similar to the Beatitudes from chapter 5?

_____

_____

_____

7. (E) Jesus now answers the disciples' question. What then does Jesus say is the greatest in the Kingdom (v. 4)?

_____

_____

_____

8. (T) In what ways can you demonstrate this kind of humility (Matthew 5:3, Philippians 2:1–11)?

_____

_____

_____

_____

9. (T) How does Jesus's teaching on humility and pride differ from the world's view today?

_____

_____

_____

Verses 5-7

10. (I) The next few chapters will be about living in community with other believers. However, in these next few verses, starting in verse 5, the word *one* is repeated. Explain how individual relationships are central to community living.

_____

_____

_____

_____

11. (I) Humility is mentioned in verses 1-4 as being greatest in the kingdom of heaven. In one word, what virtue does this section indicate is valued in the Kingdom?

_____

_____

_____

_____

12. (I) What does Jesus say would be better for a person who causes a "little one" (someone wanting to follow Christ) to sin (v. 6)? What does this reveal about Jesus's heart toward His children?

_____

_____

_____

_____

13. (T) Give an example of how someone could cause another to sin. Who does Jesus hold accountable—the tempter, the sinner, or both?

_____

_____

_____

_____

14. (T) Why do you think the consequence of leading others astray is so severe?

_____

_____

_____

_____

Verses 8-9

15. (I). In one or two words, what virtue does this section indicate is also valued in the Kingdom.

_____

_____

_____

16. (I) Read Proverbs 4:23-27, Matthew 5:29-30, 16:24, Romans 7:15-20, 12:1-2, 1 Corinthians 9:25, and 2 Corinthians 7:1. Is Jesus suggesting a literal amputation of body parts? Why or why not? What is the main point Jesus is teaching?

_____

_____

_____

_____

Verses 10-14

17. (I) How do verses 8-14 help further illustrate Matthew 7:3-5?

_____

_____

_____

18. (I) In one word, what virtue is indicated in this section?

_____

_____

_____

19. (E) What is the contrast being made between verse 10 and verse 5?

"See that you do not _____ one of these little ones." (v. 10)

"Whoever _____ one such child in my name receives me." (v. 5)

20. (I) Look up Hebrews 1:14 and note what it says the job of angels is. How does that help you understand Jesus's statement in 18:10?

_____

_____

_____

21. (I) Look more closely at the shepherd in verses 12-14–14. What does that reveal about the character and heart of the shepherd? How does this parable demonstrate your awareness of God towards His sheep?

_____

_____

_____

_____

22. (T) How does verse 14 show us more clearly what we are praying for when we pray "thy will be done" from Matthew 6:10?

_____

_____

_____

_____

23. (T) How can the Church be guilty of leaving the one sheep for dead knowing they still have many other sheep? What can you do as a follower of Christ to ensure every sheep matters?

_____

_____

_____

_____

Verses 15-17

24. (I). In one word, what virtue is this section is valued in the kingdom of heaven?

_____

_____

_____

_____

25. (E) In these verses, Jesus gives us the practical steps to follow when someone goes astray. List the four steps below.

_____

_____

_____

_____

26. (I) How does unity within God's people demonstrate the Gospel?

_____

_____

_____

_____

27. (I) How do these verses answer Cain's question in Genesis 4:9 ("Am I my brother's keeper?")?

_____

_____

_____

_____

28. (I) What is the right attitude in dealing with someone else's sin (Ephesians 4:2, Philippians 2:3)?

_____

_____

_____

_____

29. (T) Have you ever been part of a church that enforced disciplinary actions? What happened? What were some of the benefits? What are the potential risks?

_____

_____

_____

_____

_____

Verses 18-20

30. (T) We should not take excommunication lightly. What promises does Jesus make in these verses? How would these verses be an encouragement for the disciples? For the Church?

_____

_____

_____

_____

31. (I) Read Deuteronomy 19:15 and explain how the Jewish audience would have understood verse 20 in the context of church discipline.

_____

_____

_____

_____

32. (T) How is verse 20 often taken out of context? How have you heard it used before?

_____

_____

_____

_____

33. (T) What is the ultimate goal for the lost sheep in the parable and exercising church discipline? (use v. 15 to help with your answer)

_____

_____

_____

_____

Verses 21-22

34. (I) In one word, what virtue is indicated in this section?

_____

_____

_____

35. (E,I) What was Peter's question to Jesus in verse 21? How does that question logically follow Jesus's teaching in verses 15-17?

_____

_____

_____

36. (E) What was the normal practice of forgiveness among the Jews (Job 33:29, Amos 1:3, 2:6)?

_____

_____

_____

37. (I) What does Jesus's response reveal about forgiveness?

_____

_____

_____

38. (E) Why would forgiveness be valued in the kingdom of heaven?

_____

_____

_____

39. (T) How do you reconcile the tension between lavish forgiveness and placing healthy boundaries around unhealthy people?

_____

_____

_____

40. (T) Who is God placing on your heart to forgive?

_____

_____

_____

Verses 23-35

41. (I) Jesus uses a parable to further make His point with Peter. Summarize the main point in one or two sentences.

_____

_____

_____

42. (I) What do these verses reveal about the heart of the servant who had a large debt?

_____

_____

_____

43. (I) What do these verses reveal the heart of the King (God)? The Gospel?

_____

_____

_____

44. (T) Are you more often like this servant or the king? When are you most prone to demand justice rather than offer grace upon grace?

_____

_____

_____

45. (I) How does this parable demonstrate an upside-down kingdom?

_____

_____

_____

46. (E) List all the virtues or character traits we see from this chapter that should be reflected in a Kingdom citizen.

_____

_____

_____

47. (T) How does developing these character traits through the power of the Holy Spirit help us grow in Christlikeness?

_____

_____

_____

48. (T) How does humility, the greatest in the Kingdom, help with all the other traits?

_____

_____

_____

49. (I) Circle the one that best describes the point Jesus is making in this chapter.

The greatest in the kingdom of heaven is about:

Position and status

Character and heart attitude

Day 3: Read Matthew 19:1-12

Verses 1-6

1. (E) Where was Jesus heading?

_____

_____

_____

2. (E) Answer the following about the question the Pharisees asked Jesus.

What was the question?

_____

What was the motive in asking the question?

_____

Who is the initiator of the divorce?

_____

What are the limits in asking for a divorce ("for _____ cause")?

3. (I) Read Genesis 1:27-28 and Genesis 2:23-25. Why would Jesus take them all the way to the beginning to answer a question about divorce?

_____

_____

_____

_____

4. (E) Who does the "joining together" in verse 6?

_____

_____

_____

5. (I) Describe God's view on the covenant of marriage.

_____

_____

_____

Verses 7-9

6. (E) What follow-up question did the Pharisees ask?

_____

_____

_____

7. (E) Read Deuteronomy 24:1-4 and make note of your findings.

_____

_____

_____

8. (E) Verse 7 says, "Why then did Moses command one…." In verse 8, what word does Jesus use for Moses's authorization? What reason was given?

_____

_____

_____

_____

9. (I) What does the Pharisees' question reveal about their heart?

_____

_____

_____

10. (I) What is God's heart in allowing the certificate of divorce (v. 9)? How is this provision also a protection for women? (Remember that this was a culture that permitted a husband to divorce his wife for any reason.)

_____

_____

_____

11. (I) How do you reconcile God's intent for marriage (verses 1-6) and God's provision for divorce (7-9)?

_____

_____

_____

12. (I) How does our view of marriage directly relate to our view of God?

_____

_____

_____

13. (T) How is Jesus's view of commitment countercultural to today's idea of commitment?

_____

_____

_____

_____

14. (T) How could you show support and love to an individual who has been affected by divorce?

_____

_____

_____

Verses 10-12

15. (E,I) What was the disciples' response to Jesus's teaching about marriage and divorce in verse 10? What do you think about their response?

_____

_____

_____

16. (E) Read verse 11 in the Good News Translation (GNT) and fill in the blanks below.

"Jesus answered, 'This teaching does _____ , but only to those to whom _____.'"

17. (E) What does "this teaching" refer to in verse 11?

_____

_____

_____

_____

18. (T) What does verse 11 teach you about singleness/celibacy?

_____

_____

_____

_____

19. (E,I) Match the following descriptions with the words from verse 12.

Eunuchs from birth	Single/celibacy – result from a traumatic experience
Eunuchs made by men	Single/celibacy – result personal choice for God
Eunuchs for the sake of the Kingdom	Single/celibacy – result of heredity

20. (I) Do you think Jesus has a high view of singleness or not? Why do you think that?

_____

_____

_____

_____

21. (T) Name some practical ways the Church can support and embrace those who are not married.

_____

_____

_____

_____

Day 4: Read Matthew 19:13-30

Verses 13-15

1. (E) Why did the people bring children to Jesus?

_____

_____

_____

_____

2. (I) Does the response of the disciples surprise you? Why or why not?

_____

_____

_____

3. (T) What do you learn from Jesus's response?

_____

_____

_____

4. (T) How do Christians today hinder children, either literally or spiritually, from coming to Jesus?

_____

_____

_____

_____

Verses 16-22

5. (E) Fill in the blanks from the question the man asked Jesus in verse 16.

"And behold, a man came up to Him, saying, 'Teacher, what _____ must _____ to have eternal life?'"

6. (I) How did this man think a person finds eternal life?

_____

_____

_____

_____

7. (E) List the commandments Jesus specifies in verses 18-19 (Exodus 20:1-17, Leviticus 19:18).

_____

_____

_____

8. (E) Did the man believe he kept (obeyed) these commandments?

_____

_____

_____

9. (E) What two things does Jesus instruct the rich young man to do in verse 21?

_____

_____

_____

10. (I) What commandment is mentioned indirectly in verse 21 that the man was not able to keep or obey (Exodus 20:3-4)?

_____

_____

_____

11. (E) What is one purpose of the commandments (Romans 3:20)?

_____

_____

_____

_____

12. (E,I) What did the man do in verse 22? What should he have done (Matthew 3: 6, 4:17, 11:28-30)?

_____

_____

_____

13. (I) Read Romans 3:23 and James 2:10 and note what they say. Is sin external or internal?

_____

_____

_____

14. (I) Who is the only one who is good (v. 17)? Who is the only one who obeyed every law perfectly (Matthew 5:17, John 10:11, Hebrews 4:15)?

_____

_____

_____

15. (T) How does a person receive eternal life (John 3:16, Ephesians 2:8-9)?

_____

_____

_____

16. (T) In what ways do people today believe they are good and moral?

_____

_____

_____

_____

17. (T) Do you think Jesus's instructions and principles to the rich young man were intended exclusively for those in the story or meant to be relevant and applicable to all generations?

_____

_____

_____

_____

18. (T) The rich young man treasured his possessions above all things as well as believed a wrong doctrine. What treasured possession do you cling to that hinders your walk with the Lord? And, how can you transform your wrong beliefs into right theology (Psalm 119:105, John 17:17, Romans 12:2, Hebrews 4:12, 2 Timothy 3:16)?

_____

_____

_____

_____

Verses 23-26

19. (I) Why would it be difficult for a rich person to enter the Kingdom? What kind of barrier do earthly possessions hold for a rich person?

_____

_____

_____

_____

20. (I) What is the best way for a camel to go through the eye of a needle? Circle the best answer.

The camel would need a miraculous transformation.

The camel would need to work really hard.

21. (I) Why is the disciples' question in verse 25 the absolutely correct question we should all be asking?

_____

_____

_____

_____

22. (E,I) What was Jesus's response in verse 26? Who is the One who makes transformation possible? Why is this such good news?

_____

_____

_____

_____

23. (I) Paraphrase Jesus's main point in these verses. Use Ezekiel 11:19, Matthew 18:3, John 3:3, 2 Corinthians 3:18, 5:17, Ephesians 4:22-24, Galatians 2:20 to help.

_____

_____

_____

_____

Verses 27-30

24. (E) What was Peter's question in verse 27?

_____

_____

_____

_____

25. (E) Look back to Chapter 6. what is Jesus reminding them once again here in verse 28 about their reward? How is this reward greater than all earthly treasures (1 Peter 1:4)?

_____

_____

_____

_____

26. (T) Why do we, like the disciples, often need this reminder?

_____

_____

_____

_____

27. (I,T) How does verse 30 connect to the disciples' question in Matthew 18:1? How is verse 30 both an encouragement and a warning?

_____

_____

_____

_____

Day 5: Read Matthew 20

Verses 1-16

1. (E,I) Summarize the events in the parable. How is this parable a good illustration of 19:30?

_____

_____

_____

2. (I) Match the parable with the descriptions.

Master	The Kingdom
First laborers	Jesus/salvation
Last laborers	God
Vineyard	Those who respond to His call
Denarius	Gentiles
Workers in general	Jews

3. (I) Who does the going out in these verses, starting in verse 1? What does this teach us about God?

_____

_____

_____

_____

4. (E,I) What was the first laborers' complaint in verse 10? What does that reveal about their heart? What did they do in verse 11?

_____

_____

_____

_____

5. (T) Do you think they were right in being upset at the master (v. 13)? Why or why not?

_____

_____

_____

_____

6. (E,I,T) When the master replies in verse 13, what familial term does he use? What does that reveal about the character of God? How does this truth bring you comfort?

_____

_____

_____

_____

7. (E,I) What did the master reply in verse 15? What attributes of God do we see in this verse?

_____

_____

_____

_____

8. (T) What does this parable reveal about how our hearts can be when certain people come to faith in Christ. (v.12) What heart attitude should a believer have when a person comes to faith in Christ?

_____

_____

_____

_____

9. (I) How does the master demonstrate the sovereignty of God and the grace of God?

_____

_____

_____

_____

10. (T) Jesus said that the "last will be first, and the first will be last." How is this truth countercultural in the world today?

_____

_____

_____

11. (T) When was a time you received God's undeserved grace?

_____

_____

_____

Verses 17-19

12. (E,I) This is the third time Jesus tells them about the reality of His mission. Each time, Jesus adds more detail. Look up Matthew 16:21 and 17:22-23. What are the details He added in these verses?

_____

_____

_____

13. (E) What detail is mentioned in all three accounts?

"and deliver him over to the Gentiles to be mocked and flogged and crucified, and he _____."

14. (I) Why would it be important for Jesus's disciples to remember this important piece of information?

_____

_____

_____

Verses 20-23

15. (E,I) Right after Jesus talks about His suffering, what does the mother ask Jesus? Why might she have asked this (Psalm 110:1-2, Matthew 19:28-29)?

_____

_____

_____

16. (I) What question from the beginning of chapter 18 does this sound like?

_____

_____

_____

17. (E) Who are the "sons of Zebedee" (Mark 3:14-19)?

_____

_____

_____

18. (E) In response, what was Jesus's question to the mother and her sons?

_____

_____

_____

19. (E) What is the cup Jesus is referring to (Psalm 75:8, Isaiah 51:22, Jeremiah 25:15-16, Ezekiel 23:31-34)?

_____

_____

_____

20. (E) How will the sons eventually "drink the cup" (Acts 12:2, Revelation 1:9)?

_____

_____

_____

21. (T) In what way will all believers "drink the cup"?

_____

_____

_____

Verses 24-28

22. (E,I) What was the reaction of the other disciples when they heard what was asked? What do you believe motivated their reaction (18:1)?

_____

_____

_____

23. (I) According to verses 26-28, what was Jesus's cure for the longing to be great? How has this been the main point since chapter 18 (really since chapter 1)?

_____

_____

_____

24. (T) How is this principle still true for the Church today?

_____

_____

_____

25. (E) Look up the word *ransom* in a dictionary. Write a definition that best fits the context of verse 28.

_____

_____

_____

_____

26. (T) How does Jesus's message about serving others challenge you personally?

_____

_____

_____

_____

Verses 29-34

27. (I) How does the healing of the blind man illustrate the truth Jesus had just been teaching? Why is this healing a fitting closure to His teachings about the Kingdom (Isaiah 6:10, Matthew 5:8, 15:1-39)?

_____

_____

_____

_____

28. (E) What names do the blind men call Jesus?

_____

_____

_____

_____

29. (I) Describe the contrast between what the two blind men wanted and what the two brothers wanted from 20:21-23.

_____

_____

_____

_____

30. (T) In what areas of your life are you blinded by pride, seeking recognition and significance? Will you call out to the Lord today to "let your eyes be opened" and seek to serve others instead?

_____

_____

_____

_____

Day 6: Commit what you learned to prayer. Reread Matthew 18-20.

Adoration:

"God, you are…."

Pray the attributes of God we studied this week back to God.

Confession:

"Lord, I confess…."

In light of the above and what we studied this week, what did you learn about yourself?

Thanksgiving:

"Thank you…."

What from this week's passage made your heart overflow with thanksgiving?

Supplication:

"I lift up…."

After reading this week's passage, what petitions do you need to ask of God?

Global: _____

Local: _____

Personal: _____

MATTHEW 21-22

Our Actions Reveal Our Theology

AIM: Our actions reveal our theology.

Scripture to Memorize:

And he said to him, "You shall love the Lord your God with all your heart and with all your soul and with all your mind. This is the great and first commandment. And a second is like it: You shall love your neighbor as yourself."

–Matt. 22:37-39

Attribute of God: Love

Before creation, the Father, Son, and Holy Spirit loved one another. To put on display the riches of His love, God created the world and all that is in it. His love towards His children is unconditional and unfailing. It does not depend on their worth or merit. The greatest expression of His love is found in John 3:16.

Doctrine: Sanctification

To sanctify something means to set it apart for a special use. A believer's sanctification refers to a growing in holiness and Christ-like ness. It is part of a believer's salvation. Justification is a one-time, immediate, act where a person is freed from the penalty of sin. Sanctification is ongoing and gradual. It is when the Christian is freed from the power of sin. We live in a hostile world full of temptation and battle with sinful desires, but through the power of the Holy Spirit, we can learn to trust and obey and yield our thoughts, words, and actions to what pleases Him. We experience greater holiness and less sinfulness. We are not sanctified by merely trying harder. It does require disciple, but it is more about the work happening within us that overflows to our actions. John 17:17 says, "Sanctify them by the truth, your word is truth." We are changed and transformed the more we read, study, meditate, and then apply God's Word. We are a temple of the Holy Spirit and requires a pure, unadulterated dwelling place.

Sanctification is not always easy, but there should be growth happening in the believer's life. There will be signs or fruit that a person is growing in holiness such as a deep love for God's people, concern for holiness, love for God's Word, a desire to obey, and a desire to glorify God and God alone. We will not do each of these perfectly, but we should be able to recognize fruit in our lives. As we continue to pray, study the Bible, meet together in fellowship and worship with other believers, the Holy Spirit continues to do a work in us and through us. And one day we will be freed from the presence of sin when God finishes the work of salvation in our glorification.

Day 1: Read Matthew 21-22

1. In two to three sentences, summarize what happens in these chapters.

   Chapter 21

   _____

   _____

   _____

   Chapter 22

   _____

   _____

   _____

2. What is Passion Week/Holy Week?

   _____

   _____

   _____

   _____

   _____

Day 2: Read Matthew 21:1-22

Verses 1-11

1. (I) How is verse 1 the fulfillment of Zechariah 14:4?

   _____

   _____

   _____

2. (E) What two instructions does Jesus gives to two of his disciples (vv. 2-3)?

   _____

   _____

   _____

3. (I) How do these verses display both Jesus's humanity and His deity?

   _____

   _____

   _____

4. (I) Read the following passages. How are these Old Testament verses fulfilled?

   Genesis 49:10-11

   _____

   _____

   _____

   1 Kings 1:38-40

   _____

   _____

   _____

Zechariah 9:9

_____

_____

_____

5. (I) What claim is Jesus making about Himself by choosing to enter Jerusalem in this specific way (v. 5)?

    _____

    _____

    _____

6. (E,I) How is verse 5 a picture of an upside-down kingdom (Jeremiah 17:25)?

    _____

    _____

    _____

7. (I) Take a moment to meditate on verse 9. _Hosanna_ is a plea for salvation, meaning "save us or deliver us." In your own words, what was the crowd shouting?

    _____

    _____

    _____

8. (E,I) Describe the different responses to Jesus entering Jerusalem.

    The crowds:

    _____

    _____

    _____

The city:

_____

_____

_____

The disciples:

_____

_____

_____

9. (I) Explain the significance of the title "Son of David." (2 Samuel 7:12-16, Daniel 2:37, Romans 1:3, 1 Timothy 6:15, Revelation 19:16, 22:16)

_____

_____

_____

10. (T) How does this scene—the Triumphant Entry—influence your worship and devotion to Christ?

_____

_____

_____

Verses 12-13

11. (E) What is the first action Jesus takes upon entering Jerusalem?

_____

_____

_____

12. (E) Remember that the temple was the heart of Jewish worship and a representation of God's presence on earth. What does Jesus say the temple should be (v. 13)?

_____

_____

_____

13. (E) What has the temple become?

_____

_____

_____

14. (I) What do these verses reveal to us about Jesus? Does anything surprise you?

_____

_____

_____

15. (I) Read the following verses and note what they say about the spiritual temple.

Romans 12:1

_____

_____

1 Corinthians 3:16-17

_____

_____

1 Corinthians 6:19-20

_____

_____

16. (T) Read the following verses and note what they say about the connection between the purity of God's people's hearts and worship?

Psalm 51:10-12

_____

_____

Psalm 51:15-17

_____

_____

2 Corinthians 7:1

_____

_____

Philippians 4:8

_____

_____

17. (T) What kind of things pollute our personal or corporate worship? How can you give your undivided attention and time to the heart of worship?

_____

_____

_____

Verses 14-17

18. (E) What did Jesus do immediately after He drove out the "robbers"?

_____

_____

_____

19. (E) What were the two things the chief priests and scribes became angry over in verse 15?

_____

_____

_____

20. (E) Fill in the blanks with what the chief priests and scribes mention to Jesus in verse 16.

"and they said to him, Do you _____ what these are _____."

21. (E,I) Read Psalm 8:1-2. What claim is Jesus making about Himself in His response to the chief priests in v. 16? Why would this be so upsetting to the chief priests and scribes?

_____

_____

_____

Verses 18-22

22. (E) What did Jesus find (or not find) on the fig tree in verse 19?

_____

_____

_____

23. (E) What curse does Jesus pronounce on the fig tree in verse 19?

"And He said to it, 'May _____ ever come from you again!'"

24. (I) The fig tree is symbolic of Israel (Hosea 9:10, Jeremiah 24:1-8). Jesus cursed Israel for not bearing fruit. What kind of fruit was Israel to bear (Isaiah 42:6, Exodus 6:7, Deuteronomy 10:13)? Can you think of more?

_____

_____

_____

25. (E,I) Think about the main point Jesus is making. God's people are to bear fruit. This is God's will for you (Sermon on the Mount). Keeping this in mind, summarize verses 21–22 in your own words. (Review Matthew 6:10, 7:7–8.)

_____

_____

_____

_____

26. (I) How would these words (vv. 21–22) have been an encouragement for the disciples?

_____

_____

_____

_____

27. (I) What is the connection between the condition of the temple (vv. 12–16) and the fig tree?

_____

_____

_____

_____

28. (T) Re-Read 1 Corinthians 6:19–20. What internal cleansing, cultivation, and pruning from the Holy Spirit needs to happen in your life in order to produce fruit?

_____

_____

_____

_____

_____

Day 3: Read Matthew 21:23-46

Verses 23-27

1. (E) What question do the chief priests and elders ask Jesus in verse 23?

   _____

   _____

   _____

2. (I) What do you think "these things" are that the leaders are referring to?

   _____

   _____

   _____

3. (I) What do you think they are actually concerned with? (Look at the repeated word in verse 23.) Whose authority is Jesus challenging?

   _____

   _____

   _____

4. (I) Match the saying with the best understood description.

   John the Baptist baptized from heaven   His baptism a gift from God and good

   John the Baptist baptized from men   His baptism unauthorized and therefore evil

5. (I) Explain the "dilemma" the question created for the Jewish leaders (vv. 25-26).

   _____

   _____

   _____

   _____

6. (I) What is Jesus indirectly saying about the authority He has and who gave it to Him?

_____

_____

_____

7. (T) How do we as believers often challenge Jesus and His authority?

_____

_____

_____

Verses 28-32

8. (E) Describe the actions of the first son. Second son.

_____

_____

_____

9. (I) Which son correlates with the tax collectors and prostitutes? With the religious authorities?

_____

_____

_____

10. (T) Which of the two sons do you most relate to? Explain.

_____

_____

_____

_____

11. (I) Summarize in your own words the main lesson from this parable.

_____

_____

_____

Verses 33-46

12. (I) Match each of the characters with who or what they represent.

Master	Jesus
Tenants	Israel
Servants	OT prophets
Son	God
Vineyard	Jewish leaders
The other tenants	The Church

13. What does verse 33 reveal about God's heart?

_____

_____

_____

14. (I) How does this parable point us to Jesus's death?

_____

_____

_____

15. (E) Verse 41 is a very important verse. Fill in the blanks with their correlating representations from question 12 (God, Jewish leaders, Israel, the Church).

"_____ will put those _____ to a miserable death and let out _____ to _____ who will give him the fruits in their seasons."

16. (I) How do verses 42-43 further explain this point? Who is the cornerstone the builders rejected (Ephesians 2:19-22, 1 Peter 2:4-6)? What is the Lord doing (Matthew 16:18)?

_____

_____

_____

17. (T) How does this truth impact you personally?

_____

_____

_____

18. (E) What becomes clear to the chief priests and Pharisees in verse 45?

_____

_____

_____

19. (I) Read 2 Samuel 12:1-13. How is the method Jesus uses in verses 28-32 and 33-41 similar to the method Nathan used with David?

_____

_____

_____

20. (I) Read 2 Samuel 12:13. What did David do in response to God's Word? Look at the chief priest and Pharisees response in verse 46. What is the main difference between the two scenarios (Matthew 3:6,8)?

_____

_____

_____

21. (T) How can we sometimes neglect a call to repentance? Confess your sin to the Lord and ask God to cultivate the fruit of holiness in your life.

_____

_____

_____

22. (T) How can the Church be the kind of vine growers that are pleasing to God?

_____

_____

_____

Day 4: Read Matthew 22:1-40

Verses 1-14

1. (I) Match the characters in the story with who they represent.

King	Jews
Son	Salvation through Jesus
Feast	Prophets
Servants	God
Original invited guests	Gentiles
Guests invited from the city	Jesus
Wedding garment	Fellowship with God
Outer darkness	Work Salvation
The guest with the wrong garment	Hell

2. (I) From the list above, who is the most active party in this parable?

_____

_____

_____

3. (E) In what way does a particular guest offend the king in verses 11-12?

_____

_____

_____

4. (E) Read Galatians 3:27, Isaiah 61:10, Isaiah 64:6, and Romans 3:21-25. Why are the "wedding garments" so important?

_____

_____

_____

5. (T) What does this parable teach us about the judgment of God? About the kindness and patience of God? Why is it important to have a right and balanced view of both attributes?

_____

_____

_____

6. (I) Summarize in your own words the main lesson from this parable.

_____

_____

_____

7. (T) What evidence could you give that you are properly dressed in the robes of righteousness and not your own?

_____

_____

_____

_____

8. (T) What excuses do people give for rejecting Jesus? What does verse 13 say about the fate of those who reject Jesus for their salvation? What should this motivate believers to do?

_____

_____

_____

Verses 15-22

9. (E) What question did the Pharisees' disciples and Herodians ask Jesus (v. 17)?

_____

_____

_____

10. (E) What was the motive of their questioning (vv. 15, 18)?

_____

_____

_____

11. (I) Why would this question be an effective trap for Jesus (Matthew 21:17)?

_____

_____

_____

12. (E) What two things did Jesus point out to them on the denarius (v. 20)?

_____

_____

_____

13. (E) How did Jesus answer them in verse 21?

_____

_____

_____

14. (I) Read Genesis 1:26-27, Isaiah 49:16, Colossians 3:10, James 3:9, and Revelation 14:1, 19:16. Then summarize Jesus's main point in verse 21.

_____

_____

_____

15. (T) What are some things you should offer to "Caesar"? What are some things you should offer to God (Romans 13)?

_____

_____

_____

Verses 23-33

16. (I) Summarize the question the Sadducees asked Jesus in verses 23-27. (Read Deuteronomy 25:5-6 for further understanding.)

_____

_____

_____

17. (E) What were the two reasons Jesus rebuked them in verse 29?

_____

_____

_____

18. (I) Jesus answers part of their question by revealing a mystery of Heaven. What does He reveal (v.30)?

_____

_____

_____

19. (E) Fill in the blanks from verse 32.

"'I _____ the God of _____, the God of _____, and the God of _____'? He is not God of the _____, but of the _____.'"

20. (E) Who did God reveal Himself to as the "Great I Am" (Exodus 3)?

_____

_____

_____

21. (I) How does verse 32 affirm an afterlife? (Consider that "AM" is in the present tense when God spoke to Moses, but Abraham, Isaac, and Jacob would have already been dead.)

_____

_____

_____

_____

22. (I) How does Jesus's answer challenge and correct their mistaken views?

_____

_____

_____

_____

Verses 34-40

23. (E) What question did the lawyer ask Jesus in verse 36?

_____

_____

_____

24. (E) Which commandments did Jesus say are the greatest?

_____

_____

_____

25. (I) How do these commandments sum up all the Old Testament (v.40) including the 10 commandments?

_____

_____

_____

26. (T) Describe what it looks like to love God. Describe what it looks like to love your neighbor as yourself.

_____

_____

_____

27. (I) How is a right relationship with God and a right relationship with others linked? In what sense is every other commandment contingent on the greatest commandment?

_____

_____

_____

28. (T) How has someone in your life shown God's love to you recently? What specific action can you take this week to show God's love to someone?

_____

_____

_____

29. (I) Did Jesus "pass the test" of all three questions the religious leaders asked (vv. 15-40)? Why or why not?

_____

_____

_____

_____

30. (T) What do Jesus's replies reveal about Him? Did anything surprise or amaze you?

_____

_____

_____

_____

Day 5: Read Matthew 22:41-46

Verses 41-46

1. (E) What was Jesus's question to the Pharisees in verse 42?

_____

_____

_____

2. (I) What do you think was the motive or intent of Jesus's question in verses 41–42? What deeper truth was He directing the religious leaders to recognize?

    _____

    _____

    _____

3. (E,I) What was the Pharisees' answer to Jesus's question in verse 42? Were they right or wrong? How does their answer differ from Peter's answer in Matthew 16:16?

    _____

    _____

    _____

4. (I) Jesus quotes Psalm 110:1. David mentions two Lords in His psalm. The first Lord mentioned is Yahweh–God.

    Circle who best fits the second "Lord" David mentions.

    A descendant of David   The Messiah David

5. (I) Summarize the point Jesus is making in these verses. What claim is He making about Himself? Whose Son is Jesus claiming the Messiah to be?

    _____

    _____

    _____

6. (T) How has your relationship with God revealed to you a deeper understanding of who Jesus is?

    _____

    _____

    _____

7.   (T) Read verse 46 and then Job 40:1-4. How does acknowledging God's true nature lead you to "lay your hand on your mouth" over your foolish questions?

_____

_____

_____

Day 6: Commit what you learned to prayer. Reread Matthew 21-22.

Adoration:

"God, you are...."

Pray the attributes of God we studied this week back to God.

Confession:

"Lord, I confess...."

In light of the above and what we studied this week, what did you learn about yourself?

Thanksgiving:

"Thank you...."

What from this week's passage made your heart overflow with thanksgiving?

Supplication:

"I lift up...."

After reading this week's passage, what petitions do you need to ask from God?

Global: _____

Local: _____

Personal: _____

MATTHEW 23-25

God Prepares His People for His Second Coming

AIM: God prepares His people for His second coming.

Scripture to Memorize:

Therefore you also must be ready, for the Son of Man is coming at an hour you do not expect.

—Matt. 24:44

Attribute of God: Incomprehensible

We cannot fully comprehend God because He is beyond our understanding. God does want us to know Him and has revealed Himself through His creation and His Word, yet in our finite minds we cannot possibly understand an infinite being. We are too far beneath. He has revealed Himself without revealing everything there is to know about Him. We are able to only draw near to Him because He has first drawn near to us.

Doctrine: Second Coming

Jesus' second coming is the moment when He will return to save His people and to judge the living and dead. It is one of the most referenced themes in all of Scripture with over 1500 passages in the Old Testament and one in every 25 verses in the New Testament. Unlike His first coming, His second coming will be very visible and public. There will be no mistaken that it is Jesus Christ. At His ascension, He ascended into the sky and in the same way He will return. We will see the Son of Man coming on the clouds of the sky with power and great glory. It will also be very sudden and unexpected. No one knows when it will happen. We are to continue preaching the Gospel until this day happens.

For the believer, knowing Christ will return should urge us to live and conduct ourselves in a manner worthy of the Gospel of Christ. It should motivate us to live godly lives in an ungodly world. We should always be watchful, mindful, always ready and focused on heavenly things, but also not forsaking being a good steward over what God has given us to care for right now. For believers, it will be glorious day! We refer to this day as the blessed hope. We will see our Lord and Savior, be transformed, and worship Him fully in spirit and truth! The way we live will be revealed to us in that moment as well. For unbelievers, however, it will be a day of mourning and terror. Jesus's offer of salvation will be removed, and condemnation awaits those who rejected Him. They will mourn over their sin and their decision to ignore the good news but it will be too late. Jesus will return with armies at His side, evil will finally be defeated, and the Earth will be restored. And God will be glorified! For a believer, we know, our best life is yet to come.

Day 1: Read Matthew 23-25

1. In two to three sentences, summarize what happens in these chapters.

Chapter 23

_____

_____

_____

Chapter 24

_____

_____

_____

Chapter 25

_____

_____

_____

2. Why do you think people are obsessed with horoscopes, psychics, tarot cards, and more? How can studying biblical prophecy impact how we live our life today?

_____

_____

_____

_____

Day 2: Read Matthew 23

Verses 1-7

1. (E) Jesus gives instructions to the crowd and His disciples concerning the Pharisees' teachings. Answer the following questions about verse 3.

    What should they do? _____

    What should they not do? _____

    What is the reason? _____

2. (E,I) What imagery does Jesus use to describe the actions of the scribes and Pharisees in 23:4? Why is this a fitting image?

_____

_____

_____

_____

3. (I) Why would doing the works of the Pharisees be a heavy burden and hard to bear?

_____

_____

_____

_____

4. (I) What does 23:4 reveal about the Pharisees' hearts toward the people and their concern for their spiritual state?

_____

_____

_____

5. (I) Compare Jesus's words in Matthew 11:28–30 and 1 John 5:3. What do these verses say about the teachings of Christ?

_____

_____

_____

6. (E) List the evidence Jesus gives to prove His accusations (vv. 5–7).

_____

_____

_____

7. (I) What sin(s) is at the root of the religious leaders' behavior?

_____

_____

_____

8. (I) Reread Mathew 6. How is Jesus's point in these verses similar?

_____

_____

_____

Verses 8-12

9. (E,I) What transition word begins verse 8? Who two groups is Jesus contrasting?

_____

_____

_____

10. (E) Reread Matthew 20:25-26. What did the religious leaders like to "do" with their authoritative titles?

_____

_____

_____

11. (I) Do you think Jesus is literally saying that someone should not be called teacher or father? Why or why not?

_____

_____

_____

12. (E) How is Jesus instructing His disciples to behave in contrast with the Pharisees (vv. 11-12)? How is this an example of an upside-down kingdom?

_____

_____

_____

13. (I) What virtue(s) is to be reflected in a disciple of Christ?

_____

_____

_____

14. (I) Read Jeremiah 31:5. What does it tell us about God's expectations for leaders?

_____

_____

_____

15. (T) How is the Church today to regard preachers, teachers, and leaders in their congregation (1 Corinthians 12)? How can remembering this help us cultivate Jesus's point in verses 11–12?

_____

_____

_____

16. (T) How can you personally pursue serving others in your family, church, community, and the world?

_____

_____

_____

Verses 13–36

17. (I) Describe Jesus's tone in these passages. Does this surprise you? Why or why not?

_____

_____

_____

18. (E) What repeated words or phrases did you notice in each woe?

_____

_____

_____

19. Fill in the table below.

   Step 1 – Summarize each of the eight woes in one sentence.

   Step 2 – Look back to Week 3, Chapter 5, Day 2, Question 7 where you wrote a counterfeit to Jesus's blessings (what the world considers blessed). Write your answers from there below, but begin each one with "cursed." One has been done for you.

Text	Woe	Answers from Chapter 5 Week 3, Day 2, Question 7	
23:13			a
23:14 in the KJV or Mark 12:39-40			b
23:15	The Pharisees make false converts to follow and be like them, yet some become even more legalistic than they are.	Cursed are the assertive and controlling	c
23:16-22			d
23:23-24			e

Text	Woe	Answers from Chapter 5 Week 3, Day 2, Question 7	
23:25-26			f
23:27-28			g
23:29-36			h

20. (I) The words *woe* and *cursed* are interchangeable. They are declarations of eternal judgment. How do your above answers impact your thinking on how seriously God takes an unrepentant heart?

_____

_____

_____

21. (I) How do you reconcile Jesus's words and tone from these passages with His Words and tone from Matthew 5:43-48? How are we to understand and balance both His anger and His love?

_____

_____

_____

22. (T) Which of the Pharisees' traits are still common among some believers today?

_____

_____

_____

23. (I) What is the main responsibility of any spiritual leader (Matthew 3:11)?

_____

_____

_____

24. (I) Read James 3:1. How is this part of the main point Jesus is making?

_____

_____

_____

Verses 37-39

25. (I) How does Jesus's tone from 23:1-36 change in verses 37-39? What does verse 37 teach us about the heart of God? About the hearts of humans?

_____

_____

_____

26. (I) Verse 39 is a quote from Psalm 118:26. Who is the "you" Jesus is referring to in verse 39? Who is the "he" Jesus is referring to in this verse?

_____

_____

_____

27. (T) Read Deuteronomy 11:27-28. Blessings (such as the Beatitudes) and curses are both God's declaration of divine judgment. How can someone ensure that they receive His divine benediction instead of His divine anathema (Galatians 3:10-14)?

_____

_____

_____

_____

28. (T) In what ways are you prone to acknowledge only the "pleasant parts" of Jesus? How can knowing and understanding the fullness of His nature and attributes affect your worship of Him?

_____

_____

_____

_____

Day 3: Read Matthew 24

Verses 1-2

1. (E) Fill in the blanks from verse 1.

   "when the disciples came to point out to him the _____ of the _____."

2. (E) Review Matthew 23:38. What did Jesus predict would happen to the temple in these verses?

_____

_____

_____

_____

3. (I) To the disciples, this would have been hard to swallow. What would the disciples need to remember about Jesus when this happens (Matthew 12:6)?

_____

_____

_____

Verses 3–14

4. (E) What questions did the disciples ask Jesus in verse 3?

_____

_____

_____

5. (E) List the negative signs Jesus described would come before the end of the age.

vv. 4–5

_____

vv. 6–7

_____

v. 7

_____

v. 9

_____

v. 10

_____

vv. 11–12

_____

6. List the positive signs Jesus described would come before the end of the age.

v. 13

_____

v. 14

_____

7. (T) Which of these negative or positive signs can we see in the world today?

_____

_____

_____

8. (T) The repeated warning in this chapter is to beware of false teachers, prophets, and converts. Why is this caution so important (1 Peter 5:8)?

_____

_____

_____

9. (T) What do these verses teach us about God and His mission? About humanity?

_____

_____

_____

Verses 15-28

10. (E) What event did Jesus foretell in verse 15?

_____

_____

_____

11. (E) Look up the word *abomination* in a dictionary. Write a definition below. Look up the word *desolation* in a dictionary. Write a definition below.

_____

_____

_____

12. (I) Look up the following verses and write any additional information you learn about this event.

Daniel 9:27

_____

_____

_____

Daniel 11:31

_____

_____

_____

Daniel 12:11

_____

_____

_____

13. (T) The physical temple may no longer be standing, but there are still ways holy things are being desecrated today. What are some ways you can think of?

_____

_____

_____

14. (I) How does Jesus instruct His disciples to respond when the abomination of desolation happens (vv. 16-20)?

_____

_____

_____

15. (T) How is a believer to understand Jesus's instructions here about fleeing when calamity comes and His instructions in 10:30 about being willing to die for His sake?

_____

_____

_____

16. (I) Paraphrase verse 22. How would this bring the disciples hope and encouragement?

_____

_____

_____

17. (I) Jesus brings us back to the warning about those who are false in verses 23-27. What additional information about the false prophets are given in verse 24?

_____

_____

_____

18. (I) What contrast is being made in verses 26-27 concerning the coming of the Son of Man?

_____

_____

_____

Verses 29-31

19. (E) Jesus describes more signs of His return in these verses. What heavenly signs will occur?

_____

_____

_____

20. (I) What earthly signs will occur? Why do you think this will be (Matthew 13:24-30, 36-43)?

_____

_____

_____

21. (E) The Old Testament prophets use similar language to describe Jesus's return. Write some below that you find.

Isaiah 13:9-10

_____

_____

_____

22. Match the differences between Jesus's first coming and His second coming.

First coming   Dramatic, obvious, in the sky

Second coming   Quiet, obscure, on earth

23. (T) Do these verses encourage you or frighten you? Why?

_____

_____

_____

_____

Verses 32-35

24. (E) Fill in the blanks from verse 34.

    "Truly, I say to you, _____ will not pass away until all these things take place."

25. (I) Circle your best interpretation of "this generation" you think Jesus is referring to in verse 34. (Many distinguishable scholars differ on the interpretation of this particular verse.)

    Circle One: Circle One:

    Believers   living at the time of Jesus's ministry

    Unbelievers   living at some other later date in time

    Jews   a combination of both times

    All people

    Evil religious leaders

26. (E,T) What does Jesus say is perishable in verse 35? Imperishable? How is this truth still relevant today? What other perishable and imperishable things can you think of?

    _____

    _____

    _____

    _____

    _____

27. (I) What do you think is the main lesson(s) Jesus is teaching His disciples with the illustration of the fig tree?

    _____

    _____

    _____

    _____

    _____

Verses 36-51

28. (E) What does verse 36 teach about the date and exact time of Jesus's second coming?

_____

_____

_____

_____

29. (I) Fill in the chart below to help better understand Jesus's teaching on the nature of His return and the response between true believers and unbelievers. The first one has been done for you.

Text	The People	The Contrast	Their Focus	Main Point
24:37-39 (and Genesis 6-7)	Noah The people	Building an ark Eating, drinking, marrying	Heavenly focus Earthly focus	Be watchful and mindful. Do not be unaware of the coming judgment.
24:40-44	Two men in the field Two women in the field		(many scholars differ on this. Write your best guess.)	
24:45-51	Faithful and wise servant Wicked servant			

30. (T) What is the message for believers today?

_____

_____

_____

31. (T) What earthly distractions can cause you to lose heavenly focus? How can you practice a healthy watchfulness of Christ's return in your everyday routines?

_____

_____

_____

_____

Day 4: Read Matthew 25

Verses 1-13

1. (I) What main theme is carried over from Matthew 24:36-41 to these verses (v. 13)?

_____

_____

_____

_____

2. (I) Draw a line matching each element from the story to what it represents.

5 wise virgins	Jesus Christ
5 foolish virgins	Readiness and alertness
Lamps	Eternal fellowship with God
Bridegroom	Faithful and blessed servants
Marriage feast	Unfaithful and cursed servants

3. (E) What was the eternal fate for the five wise virgins? The five foolish virgins?

_____

_____

_____

4. (T) What reassurance does this parable provide about your relationship to the Bridegroom, Jesus Christ?

_____

_____

_____

Verses 14–30

5. (I) Draw a line matching each element from the story to what it represents.

Man going on a journey	What God has entrusted to us
Talent	Faithful servant
Servants who had five and two talents	Jesus Christ
Servant who received one talent	Unfaithful servant
Outer darkness	Hell

6. (I) Describe the attitude of the servants in response to the master's allotment.

_____

_____

_____

7. (E,I) What does the master say to the servant to whom he gave the five talents (v. 21)? The two talents (v. 23)? What does this teach us?

"Well _____, _____ and _____ servant!"

8. (E) Take a close look at verses 24-25. How does the servant view his master?

_____

_____

_____

9. (E) Who does the servant blame for his misuse of the talent?

_____

_____

_____

10. (T) What was the eternal fate for the servants given five and two talents? For the servant given one talent?

_____

_____

_____

11. (T) What spiritual gift or talent has God given you, and how are you using them to bless others?

_____

_____

_____

12. (T) How would you explain the parable of the talents to a new Christian?

_____

_____

_____

_____

Verses 31-40

13. (I) Describe the scene when the Son of Man comes in His glory.

_____

_____

_____

14. (I) How is this parable similar to Matthew 13:24–30, 47-50?

_____

_____

_____

15. (E) Who separates the sheep from the goats?

_____

_____

_____

16. (E) Fill in the chart.

	Who are they?	Where are they placed?	What does Jesus call them?	Eternal Fate?
Sheep			(v. 34)	(v. 46)
Goats			(v. 41)	

17. (E) What did the righteous do (vv. 35-36) that the unrighteous did not (vv. 42-43)?

_____

_____

_____

18. (I) Salvation is not earned by a person's deeds but explains how a person's deeds are a reflection of what is in their heart (Luke 6:45, James 2:14-17, 1 John 3:16-18).

_____

_____

_____

19. (E) What confused "the sheep" in verses 37-39?

_____

_____

_____

20. (E) How did Jesus respond to them in verse 40?

_____

_____

_____

_____

21. (T) How is this still true for believers today?

_____

_____

_____

_____

22. (T) Jesus makes it clear that the most important thing we are entrusted with are people, especially the "least of these." Read His parables in light of this truth. How does this truth impact you personally?

_____

_____

_____

23. (I) This week was the final of Jesus's five discourses. Give a title, write a brief summary, and give the main points for each discourse (Matthew 5-7, 10, 13, 18, 24-25).

_____

_____

_____

_____

Day 5: Read Matthew 23-25

1. (T) Are you ready for Jesus to return? What specific changes do you need to make in your life in light of the truths found in these chapters? How would you respond if Jesus asked you, "Why should you receive eternal life?"

_____

_____

_____

_____

Day 6: Commit what you learned to prayer. Reread Matthew 23-25.

Adoration:

"God, you are…."

Pray the attributes of God we studied this week back to God.

Confession:

"Lord, I confess…."

In light of the above and what we studied this week, what did you learn about yourself?

Thanksgiving:

"Thank you…."

What from this week's passage made your heart overflow with thanksgiving?

Supplication:

"I lift up…."

After reading this week's passage, what petitions do you need to ask from God?

Global: _____

Local: _____

Personal: _____

MATTHEW 26

Jesus, the Guarantor of a Better Covenant

AIM: Jesus, the guarantor of a better covenant.

Scripture to Memorize:

For this is My blood of the covenant, which is poured out for many for the forgiveness of sins.

–Matt. 26:28

Attribute of God: Sovereign

God controls all things. There is nothing in the universe that occurs without His permission. He has the power and authority to do anything He chooses with His creation. Whatever God plans, He will accomplish because He alone has the power. No circumstance, person, not even Satan can thwart His plans. Nothing in this world can happen apart from divine sovereignty. Evil exists because God permits it, and we can find comfort knowing it will be used for His people's good and His glory. We only need to look at the cross.

Doctrine: The New Covenant

The basic structure of the relationship God has established with His people is the covenant. It is a binding agreement between two parties with principles and guidelines. In the Old Testament, the Abrahamic Covenant promised Abraham many descendants and a great nation would come from him, and they would be a blessing to the world. The Mosaic Covenant was a conditional covenant that either brought God's blessing or curse depending on the obedience of Israel. The Davidic Covenant promised a kingly descendant who would sit on the throne forever and rule an eternal kingdom.

The New Covenant fulfills everything that was promised in the earlier covenants God made. It is unconditional and dependent on Him alone to keep the terms. In the Old Covenant, it was necessary for a prophet, priest, or king to share a revelation about the knowledge of God. In the New Covenant, the one true prophet, priest, and king- Jesus Christ is the full revelation of God, Himself. When we come to know Him, we will know God. He is the mediator and brings spiritual blessings such as a new heart and the forgiveness of sins. It is this new heart that is at the center of the covenant. In the Old Covenant, the law was placed inside the ark of the covenant, but in the New the law will be written on the hearts of God's people. Through the power of the Holy Spirit in us, a desire to live in fellowship with God will be "rewritten" on our heart just like in the Garden with Adam. Obedience would be internal. Covenants are ratified with blood; half the blood would be on the altar and the other half on the people to make atonement and to purify or sanctify. The animal blood from the Old Covenant pointed to the blood Jesus spilled on our behalf to make atonement for sin and our justification. It was through His death, the New Covenant was consecrated.

Day 1: Read Matthew 26

1. In two to three sentences, summarize what happens in this chapter.

   Chapter 26

   _____

   _____

   _____

2. Underline every time the words *betray*, *handed over*, or *delivered* occur in this chapter. How many times do they occur?

   Matthew is connecting these words to the language of the Old Testament, especially in the book of Judges. Read Judges 6:1 in the NKJV. Make note of who does the delivering in this verse. Now read Genesis 50:20. What do you think Matthew wants us to remember as we read chapter 26 (who really is the one in charge)?

   _____

   _____

   _____

   _____

Day 2: Read Matthew 26:1-16

Verses 1-5

1. (E) Verse 1 says, "when Jesus had finished all these sayings." What are all these sayings that are being referenced?

   _____

   _____

   _____

2. (E) What new detail does Jesus add this time about His crucifixion in verse 2?

   _____

   _____

   _____

3. (E) What were the chief priests and elders doing in verses 3-4?

   _____

   _____

   _____

4. (I) Look up the word *stealth* and write a definition that best fits the way it is used in verse 4. Who does this bring to mind (Genesis 3:1)?

   _____

   _____

   _____

   _____

5. (E) Fill in the blanks from verse 5.

   "But they said, 'Not _____, lest there be an uproar among the people.'"

Verses 6-13

6. (E) The chief priests and elders were gathered in a palace of the high priest. Contrast that with the setting from verse 6.

_____

_____

_____

7. (E) Summarize the events that happened in these verses.

_____

_____

_____

8. (I) What is significant about what the woman did (1 Samuel 9:15-16, 16:12-13, 1 Kings 1:38-40)?

_____

_____

_____

9. (E,I) What was the disciples' response to the woman's actions in verses 8-9? Was the disciples' concern for the poor right or wrong (Deuteronomy 15:4-11)?

_____

_____

_____

10. (I) Paraphrase Jesus's response to them in verses 10-13.

_____

_____

_____

11. (I) Review Matthew 13:44-46. How is this woman an example of living out these parables?

_____

_____

_____

12. (I) Explain in your own words why the actions of the woman are so meaningful that Jesus says she is to be remembered for all time.

_____

_____

_____

13. (T) What sacrifice have you offered to the Lord that was costly?

_____

_____

_____

_____

Verses 14-16

14. (E) Fill in the blanks from verse 14.

"Then _____, whose name was _____ to the chief priests."

15. (E,I) John 12:4-6 gives us a little more insight into Judas and his actions. What do these verses reveal about him (Matthew 6:24)?

_____

_____

_____

_____

16. (I) What is significant about the amount Judas was paid (Exodus 21:32, Zechariah 11:12-13)?

_____

_____

_____

17. (I) Contrast the scene with the woman from verse 7 with the Judas scene from these verses. What do their actions reveal about their contrasting views of who Jesus is?

_____

_____

_____

_____

Day 3: Read Matthew 26:17-30

Verses 17-19

1. (E) What Jewish feast did Jesus and His disciples prepare to celebrate?

_____

_____

_____

_____

2. (I) Write everything you know about the Passover—the significance, the events, the yearly celebration, and so on.

_____

_____

_____

_____

3. (E) What instructions does Jesus give His disciples in preparation for this important celebration?

_____

_____

_____

4. (E) How did the disciples respond to Jesus's request?

_____

_____

_____

Verses 20-25

5. (E) What bombshell did Jesus drop on the disciples in verse 21?

_____

_____

_____

6. (I) Look up the word *betray* in the dictionary and write a definition for it that best fits the way it is used in these verses.

_____

_____

_____

7. (I) Jesus mentions that someone will betray Him several times before revealing who it is in verse 25. Why do you think He did that? What attribute of Jesus does this demonstrate?

_____

_____

_____

8. (E) How did the disciples respond to this news?

    _____

    _____

    _____

9. (E) Who will be the one to betray Jesus?

    _____

    _____

    _____

10. (T) In what sense are we all like Judas and have betrayed the Son of Man?

    _____

    _____

    _____

11. (I) How do we see both Jesus's humanity and deity in this passage?

    _____

    _____

    _____

Verses 26-30

12. (I) List all the ways Jesus connects the significance of the meal to Himself. What is the significance of each way?

    _____

    _____

    _____

    _____

13. (I) Write as many similarities and differences as possible between the Passover meal and the Last Supper.

_____

_____

_____

_____

14. (I) Compare verse 28 with Matthew 1:21. What do these verses say about the mission of Christ?

_____

_____

_____

_____

15. (I) Covenants are ratified with divided flesh and the spilled blood of a sacrifice (Genesis 15:9-10, Exodus 24:6-8). Whose body will be ripped apart? Whose blood with be spilled for the remission of sins? Who will be offered as the perfect sacrificial lamb (Isaiah 53)?

_____

_____

_____

_____

16. (I) Explain how the Last Supper is a visible, outward picture pointing to the invisible, internal reality of the New Covenant.

_____

_____

_____

_____

17. (I) How does our modern day Lord's Supper have a past, present, and future reality (1 Corinthians 11:26)?

_____

_____

_____

_____

18. (T) Why is personal faith in Christ necessary to fully understand, participate in, and celebrate the Lord's Supper?

_____

_____

_____

_____

19 (T) What modern-day lessons does this section teach us about coming to the Lord's Supper (Use 1 Corinthians 11:27–32 to help with answer)?

_____

_____

_____

_____

20. (T) How can you prepare yourself better to partake of the Lord's Supper to make it more meaningful and beneficial to you?

_____

_____

_____

_____

_____

21. (E) Fill in the blanks from verse 30. What was their response to everything they just saw and heard? (Read Ephesians 5:17-21 for a deeper understanding.)

"And when they had _____ a _____, they went out to the Mount of Olives."

_____

_____

_____

Day 4: Read Matthew 26:31-56

Verses 31-56

1. (I) Jesus will now live out the Beatitudes (Matthew 5) in the Garden of Gethsemane. Place a verse (from verses 31-56) next to each Beatitude where you think He best demonstrates each one. I did one for you.

Blessed are the poor in spirit _____

Blessed are those that mourn _____

Blessed are the meek _____

Blessed are those who hunger and thirst for righteousness _____

Blessed are the merciful _____

Blessed are the pure in heart _____

Blessed are the peacemakers _____verse 52_____

Blessed are those who are persecuted for righteousness' sake _____

Verses 31-35

2. (E) What three significant events does Jesus predict in verses 31-34 (Zechariah 13:7)?

_____

_____

_____

_____

3. (I) Describe the response of Peter and the disciples in verses 33 and 35. What word does Peter use in verse 33 ("I will _____ fall away")?

    _____

    _____

    _____

    _____

4. (T) What lessons can you learn from the response of Peter and the other disciples?

    _____

    _____

    _____

    _____

5. (T) In what ways do you often strive to follow the Lord but are tempted to rely on your own strength to do it?

    _____

    _____

    _____

    _____

Verses 36-39

6. (I) Read Genesis 2 and 22. What Old Testament main stories does Matthew want to connect to these next few verses?

    _____

    _____

    _____

    _____

7. (E,I) What did Jesus say He was going to do in verse 36? What lesson can we learn from that?

    _____

    _____

    _____

    _____

8. (E) Who does Jesus take with Him to the Garden of Gethsemane (v. 37)? Where else have we seen this specific trio (Matthew 17)?

    _____

    _____

    _____

    _____

9. (I) In what ways does Jesus's struggle in the Garden of Gethsemane reveal both His humanity and His deity?

    _____

    _____

    _____

    _____

10. (I) Jesus says His "soul is very sorrowful, even to death" because (v. 39) He is about to "drink the cup." In your own words, what is the cup referring to (Jeremiah 25:15-16, Isaiah 51:17, Revelation 14:10)? How does drinking this cup contribute to His intense sorrow?

    _____

    _____

    _____

    _____

11. (E,I) Write below the prayer from verse 39. How is this prayer similar to His prayer in Matthew 6:9-15?

_____

_____

_____

12. (T) How is Jesus's prayer in the Garden of Gethsemane an example to us? What should we understand from "not as I will, but as you will"?

_____

_____

_____

13. (T) Is there a current situation where you need to complete a prayer with "not as I will, but as you will"? Will you pray it to God right now?

_____

_____

_____

Verses 40-46

14. (I,E) In verse 40, did the disciples fulfill Jesus's request from verse 36? How many times did they fail?

_____

_____

_____

15. (E) In verse 41, what reason did Jesus give to the disciples who were to watch and pray.

"Watch and pray that you may not _____."

16. (E,I) Who is the tempter (1 Peter 5:8, James 1:13)? How does this scene give insight into the foreboding reality of spiritual battles?

_____

_____

_____

17. (T) How does praying help God's people "not enter into temptation"?

_____

_____

_____

18. (I) What do you notice about the progression of submission in Jesus's prayer in vv.39, 42, 46?

_____

_____

_____

19. (T) Knowing God strengthens us when we pray and knowing temptation is defeated through prayer, why is prayer such a struggle for many Christians?

_____

_____

_____

Verses 47-56

20. (E) How did Judas, the crowd, chief priests, and elders approach Jesus in verse 47?

_____

_____

_____

21. (E) Fill in the blanks from verse 49 and then Jesus's response in verse 50.

"And he [Judas] came up to Jesus at once and said, 'Greetings, _____!' And he _____ him."

"Jesus said to him, '_____, do what you came to do.'"

22. (E,I) Take a closer look at verse 50. When did "they" seize Jesus? Circle the correct answer. What do we learn about the authority of Jesus from this account?

Before Jesus gave the command

While Jesus was giving the command

After Jesus gave the command

23. (I) How does Jesus's words in verse 52 express that His Kingdom is an upside-down kingdom?

_____

_____

_____

_____

_____

24. (I) Paraphrase verses 52-56. What is Jesus's main point (look for the repeated phrase in verses 54 and 56)?

_____

_____

_____

_____

_____

25. Fill in the blanks from verse 56. How is the verse a fulfillment of Jesus's words from verse 31?

"Then all the _____ him and _____."

26. (T) This section reveals the vulnerabilities, fears, and weaknesses of all the disciples. What steps can you take to protect yourself against the same (hint: vv. 40–46 and Ephesians 6:10-18)?

_____

_____

_____

Day 5: Read Matthew 26:57-75

Verses 57-68

1. (E) Where was Jesus taken, and who was present?

_____

_____

_____

2. (I) Based on the text, were the Sanhedrin (ruling council of Jews) seeking the truth about Jesus? Why or why not?

_____

_____

_____

_____

3. (E,I) What testimony do the witnesses give about Jesus in verse 61? Was it a true witness? (Read John 2:13–22.)

_____

_____

_____

_____

4. (I) Read Deuteronomy 17:6. What is significant about the two witnesses?

_____

_____

_____

5. (I,T) Read Isaiah 53:7. How is this prophecy fulfilled in Jesus's response (v. 63) to the first question of the high priest? What do you learn from His response?

_____

_____

_____

6. (E) What question did the high priest ask Jesus after His silence in verse 63? Why is this question essential?

_____

_____

_____

_____

7. (E) What statement does Jesus make that infuriates the Sanhedrin (v. 64)? Read Psalm 110:1, Daniel 7:13-14, and Revelation 1:7. What do you learn from Jesus's reply to Caiaphas?

_____

_____

_____

_____

8. (E) Fill in the blank. What was their judgment for Jesus (v. 66)?

"He _____."

9. (I) As the religious leaders were taunting Jesus about a prophecy, they were actually fulfilling one. Read Isaiah 50:5-6. How is Isaiah's prophecy fulfilled in Christ and the religious leaders?

_____

_____

_____

Verses 69-75

10. (E) Who approaches Peter about his relationship to Jesus in verses 69, 71, and 73?

_____

_____

_____

11. (I) Why do you think Peter lies about knowing Jesus?

_____

_____

_____

12. (I) Place the following statements in the correct order of progression.

    Peter invokes a curse on himself and swears he does not know Jesus.

    Peter says he does not know Jesus.

    Peter swears with an oath that he does not know Jesus.

13. (I) Compare the attitudes and actions of Judas and Peter. Do you think they will receive the same eternal consequences? Why or why not? What makes the difference?

_____

_____

_____

14. (T) Peter denies Jesus three times, just as Jesus predicted. In what ways can we also deny our relationship with Christ either intentionally or unintentionally?

_____

_____

_____

_____

15. (T) How does knowing Jesus's _yes_ to Peter is greater than Peter's _no_ to Him bring you comfort and peace of mind?

_____

_____

_____

_____

Day 6: Commit what you learned to prayer. Reread Matthew 26.

Adoration:

"God, you are…."

Pray the attributes of God we studied this week back to God.

Confession:

"Lord, I confess…."

In light of the above and what we studied this week, what did you learn about yourself?

Thanksgiving:

"Thank you…."

What from this week's passage made your heart overflow with thanksgiving?

Supplication:

"I lift up...."

After reading this week's passage, what petitions do you need to ask of God?

Global: _____

Local: _____

Personal: _____

MATTHEW 27

Jesus Is the Better, Once and for All Sacrifice

AIM: Jesus is the better, once and for all sacrifice.

Scripture to Memorize:

And behold, the curtain of the temple was torn in two, from top to bottom. And the earth shook, and the rocks were split.

–Matt. 27:51

Attribute of God: Wrath

God hates sin and all that dishonors Him. God's wrath is a righteous and holy response to something outside of Himself. Sin and disobedience bring the wrath of God, and we are all sinners. God is love but acts in wrath against all who violate His love. It is not the same as human anger. It does not include getting even or the idea of paying back. It is always perfectly just. Jesus suffered the full extent of God's wrath when He hung on the cross. He experienced what we deserve so we can experience the fullness of Him.

Doctrine: Substitution

Substitutionary atonement is the essence of the Gospel. It is the very heart of Christianity. All Scripture points to the Savior who would come and lay down His life to take away the sins of His people. Substitutionary Atonement refers to Jesus Christ dying on behalf of sinners. He is the only acceptable sacrifice for sin. There is no other name under Heaven by which we must be saved. We cannot save ourselves; we need a substitute to take our place.

We are all sinners and the wages of sin is death. Without Christ we will spend an eternity in hell as payment for our sins. Those who fail to accept Jesus, will bear the weight of their own judgment. They will face everlasting torment. They will have the full wrath of God upon them forever. For those who believe Jesus took our place will stand before God and though guilty, we will be declared innocent. He willingly did all this on our behalf. All His suffering and affliction was for us. This is because Jesus loves us. The curse and death He took upon the cross was really ours. We deserved to be the ones on the cross to die because we are the ones who live sinful lives. But, He took our punishment and gave us His righteousness in exchange. He satisfied the payment due for sinfulness of man. This is why we can have peace with God. Because of what He did, we now can have our sins forgiven and are able to spend eternity with Him forever. Jesus was bound and pronounced guilty so the guilty could be set free and be pronounced forgiven. The gift of God is eternal life in Christ Jesus our Lord. This truly is good news, indeed. Praise God.

Day 1: Read Matthew 27

1. In two to three sentences, summarize what happens in this chapter.

   Chapter 27

   _____

   _____

   _____

2. Where do you see the sovereignty of God in this chapter?

   _____

   _____

   _____

Day 2: Read Matthew 27:1-10

Verses 1-2

1. (E) Jesus is taken to Pontius Pilate. Who was he? Was he Jewish or Roman/Gentile? Read John 18:29-31 and note what Pilate can do that the religious leaders cannot.

   _____

   _____

   _____

2. (I) How are these verses a fulfillment of Psalm 2?

_____

_____

_____

Verses 3–10

3. (E) Fill in the blanks from verse 3.

   "Then when Judas, His betrayer, saw that Jesus was condemned, He _____ and brought back the thirty pieces of silver."

4. (I) Read verse 3 in the NKJV. What differences do you notice?

_____

_____

_____

5. (E) What does Judas confess to the chief priests and elders in verse 4? What does he do in verse 5?

_____

_____

_____

_____

6. (I) Do you think Judas' actions in these verses reflect a desire for forgiveness and true repentance? Why or why not?

_____

_____

_____

_____

7. (E) What was the chief priests' and elders' response to Judas in verse 4?

_____

_____

_____

8. (I) What does that reveal about their hearts?

_____

_____

_____

9. (T) In what ways can the church be like the Pharisees and too dismissive when someone is wanting to confess their guilt?

_____

_____

_____

10. (E) What did the chief priests and elders do with the money?

_____

_____

_____

_____

11. (I) How is this section a fulfillment of Jeremiah 19:1-13 and Zechariah 11:12-13?

_____

_____

_____

_____

12. (E) Read Deuteronomy 27:25 and then fill in the blanks from verse 6. Is this a true or false statement?

    "_____ to put them into the treasury, since it is blood money."

13. (I) What is the chief priests' main concern, saving the life of Jesus or obeying the law? How is this an example of "I desire mercy, not sacrifice" -what Jesus has been rebuking them for throughout the Gospel of Matthew (see Matthew 9:13)?

    _____

    _____

    _____

    _____

    _____

14. (I) Compare and contrast the attitudes, actions, and responses of Peter (Matthew 26:69-75) and Judas.

    _____

    _____

    _____

    _____

    _____

15. (T) How can knowing who God is help with our battle for sin? How can it help restore and not destroy our relationship with Him and others?

    _____

    _____

    _____

    _____

    _____

Day 3: Read Matthew 27:11-31

Verses 11-14

1. (E,I) What question did Pilate ask Jesus? Why do you think he asked that particular question?

    _____

    _____

    _____

2. (I) Compare Pilate's question to the question the Jewish council asked in 26:63.

    _____

    _____

    _____

    _____

3. (I) How is Jesus's behavior before Pilate similar to His behavior before the high priest in the previous chapter (26:62-62, 27:12-14)? How is this a fulfillment of Isaiah 53:7 and Psalm 38:13-15?

    _____

    _____

    _____

    _____

4. (E) How did Pilate respond to Jesus's behavior in verse 14?

    _____

    _____

    _____

    _____

5. (I) Read the following verses. How did Jesus exemplify wisdom in remaining to be silent?

Psalm 39:1

_____

Proverbs 10:19

_____

Proverbs 12:6

_____

Proverbs 18:21

_____

Ecclesiastes 3:7

_____

Ecclesiastes 5:2

_____

Matthew 12:36-37

_____

Colossians 4:6

_____

James 3:1-12

_____

6. (T) Describe a time in your life when you sought justice for yourself instead of remaining silent. What was the result?

_____

_____

Verses 15-26

7.   (I) Summarize what is happening in these verses.

_____

_____

_____

_____

8.   (E) What custom did the Roman governor observe during the Jewish Passover (v. 15)?

_____

_____

_____

_____

9.   (E) Who was the prisoner brought before the crowd? Read Mark 15:6-7. Why was he in prison?

_____

_____

_____

_____

_____

10. (E) Pilate was aware of the motive behind Jesus being delivered up. What was it (v. 18)?

_____

_____

_____

_____

11. (T) Envy is a dangerous and serious sin, manifesting as early as the Garden of Eden. Identify a specific instance where you have been envious. What does that instance reveal about your fleshly needs or desires? How does understanding God's goodness and sovereignty help with our struggle with covetousness?

_____

_____

_____

12. (E) What other warning did Pilate receive (v. 19)?

_____

_____

_____

_____

13. (E) What was the crowd's stated desire for Jesus in vv.21,22, and 23?

_____

_____

_____

_____

14. (E) Fill in the blank. What was Pilate's question to the crowd in verse 23?

"Why? What _____"

15. (E) What had Jesus been doing for the crowds (Matthew 11:4-5)? List them below.

_____

_____

_____

_____

16. (,I) What does this teach us about human nature in general?

_____

_____

_____

17. (I) Pilate claimed to be "innocent of this man's blood" in verse 24. Is this statement true or false? Explain your answer.

_____

_____

_____

18. (I) Write verse 25 in your own words. How is this verse the whole point of the story?

_____

_____

_____

19. (E) Match the account on the left with the individuals in the middle. Then match the account on the right with the correct individual in the middle. (Read Mark 15:6-7 to help with the answer.)

Guilty   Barabbas   Chained

Innocent   Jesus   Set free

20. (I) In what ways does the release of Barabbas illustrate a believer's release from judgment (check the doctrine)? How is this exchange already pointing forward to the cross?

_____

_____

_____

21. (T) What lessons do you learn from Pilate and his actions to the crowd and Jesus?

_____

_____

_____

22. (T) How easily are you influenced by public opinion? What precautions can you take to ensure you do not go along with the crowd?

_____

_____

_____

Verses 27-31

23. (E) List all the physical torment and emotional suffering Jesus endured in these verses, including the one from verse 26.

_____

_____

_____

24. (T) How does this truth impact you personally?

_____

_____

_____

25. (I) Read Isaiah 50:6. How does this verse find fulfillment in Christ?

_____

_____

_____

26. (I) Compare this section to Jesus's words in Matthew 5:10. How is Jesus living out His teachings?

_____

_____

_____

27. (I) Compare the first part of verse 28 to Genesis 3:21. What is the spiritual significance of Adam being covered and clothed and Jesus being stripped bare? How does this point us to the truth that Jesus the true and better Adam (read Genesis 3:6–21 for more context)?

_____

_____

_____

28. (I) Compare verse 29 to Philippians 2:10–11. The soldiers were mocking Jesus's kingship, but their actions are almost like a prophecy. How do their actions point to a deeper and greater truth that is to come?

_____

_____

_____

Day 4: Read Matthew 27:32-53

Verses 32-37

1. (I) What four words are at the beginning of verse 32? Read Leviticus 4:12, 21 and Hebrews 13:11-12. What is significant about the meaning of these four words? How is this another fulfillment of Old Testament prophecy?

_____

_____

_____

2. (E,I) What did Jesus need help carrying? How does this demonstrate His humanity?

_____

_____

_____

3. (E,I) What did they offer Jesus in verse 34? How is that a fulfillment of Psalm 69:20-21?

_____

_____

_____

4. (I) Look up the definition of *crucifixion* and write it below. Then read Deuteronomy 21:22-23 and write the significance about what is happening.

_____

_____

_____

5. (E,I) What were the soldiers doing in verse 35? How is this a fulfillment of Psalm 22:18?

_____

_____

_____

6. (E,I) Write verse 36 below. What is ironic about this verse? (Who is "keeping watch over" whom?)

_____

_____

_____

_____

7. (I) Was the charge placed over Jesus's head true or false (v. 37)? Once again, a deep truth is being preached through reproach. What is significant about the charge?

    _____

    _____

    _____

    _____

8. (T) Take some time to meditate on what Jesus was willing to go through and that He knew what was going to happen next. What are your thoughts on the fact that He was willing to go through it all in order to save people—including you—from their sins?

    _____

    _____

    _____

    _____

Verses 38-44

9. (I) How is verse 38 a fulfillment of Isaiah 53:12?

    _____

    _____

    _____

    _____

10. (I) What is the spiritual significance of Jesus being crucified between the two thieves (Romans 6:4, 2 Corinthians 5:21, 1 Peter 2:24, 3:18, Hebrews 4:14-16)?

    _____

    _____

    _____

    _____

11. (E) List the three groups of scoffers in verses 39, 41, and 44.

_____

_____

_____

_____

12. (I) How are verses 39–40 a fulfillment of Psalm 22:7-8?

_____

_____

_____

_____

13. (I) Fill in the blanks from verse 40.

"_____, come down from the cross."

14. (E,I) Who else uttered those words from Matthew 4:1-11? How is this temptation through mocking similar to the way Satan tempted Jesus in Matthew 4:1-11?

_____

_____

_____

_____

15. (I) Compare 27:40 with Matthew 16:24-25. How do you see Jesus living out His earlier words in this section?

_____

_____

_____

_____

16. (E) What four true statements did the religious leaders taunt Jesus with in verses 42–43?

_____

_____

_____

_____

17. (T) We often want to disassociate ourselves with the men and women who committed these terrible acts against Jesus, but why should we be careful not to do that?

_____

_____

_____

_____

Verses 45–50

18. (E) List three events that happened preceding Jesus's death in verses 45, 46, and 47.

_____

_____

_____

_____

19. (I) The darkness in the middle of the day is a physical manifestation of a spiritual truth (Genesis 1:2, Exodus 10:22, Micah 7:8, Matthew 4:16, John 9:5, Ephesians 5:8). What is the deeper and underlying spiritual message that is happening here (Isaiah 13:9–10, Acts 2:20)?

_____

_____

_____

_____

20. (I) Read Habakkuk 1:13 and 2 Corinthians 5:21. Paraphrase what is happening in verse 46. How is verse 46 a fulfillment of Psalm 22:1?

_____

_____

_____

21. (I) For a better understanding of the curse the Father inflicted on Jesus and what He endured on the cross on our behalf, read it as the opposite of one of God's blessings. Read the Jewish blessing found in Numbers 6:24-26 and then replace the missing words with their antonym provided in the word box. One has been done for you.

The Lord _____ you and _____ you; the Lord _____ keep you in darkness and _____; the Lord _____ toward you and _____.

Word Box:	
Abandon	curse
Keep you in darkness	turn his back
Judge without grace	remove his peace

22. (T) What emotion does Jesus's last words evoke in you?

_____

_____

_____

23. (I) Simon of Cyrene needed to bare Jesus's cross, but Jesus on the cross bore Simon's sin. How does this demonstrate Jesus's deity?

_____

_____

_____

24. (E,I) What is significant about the strangers' actions in verses 48–49 (Matthew 5:7, 25:31–40)?

_____

_____

_____

25. (E) Fill in the blanks from verse 50.

"And Jesus cried out again with a loud voice and _____."

26. (I) Read verses 45 and 50, along with Genesis 1:1-3, 2 Corinthians 5:17, and John 1:1-18, 11:25-26. Paraphrase the core spiritual and cosmic truth that is happening. How is life and order brought forth from death and chaos?

_____

_____

_____

27. (I) Contrast the fact Jesus died on Passover with the words of the chief priests and elders from 26:5. What does this teach us about God's plans, purposes, and sovereignty?

_____

_____

_____

_____

28. (I) What is the spiritual significance of Jesus dying on the Passover? (Exodus 12:5-23, John 1:29, 1 Corinthians 5:7, Hebrews 9:12, 1 Peter 1:19, Revelation 5:6)

_____

_____

_____

_____

29. (T) How does Jesus's death on the cross give you insight into the depravity of your sin and the costly price He paid for your redemption?

_____

_____

_____

_____

30. (T) How will you view Jesus's death on the cross differently after studying it this week?

_____

_____

_____

_____

Verses 51-53

31. (I) What three signs did God give following Jesus's death (vv. 51-52)?

_____

_____

_____

_____

32. (E) Read the following verses and paraphrase the significance of the torn veil.

Leviticus 16

_____

_____

Isaiah 59:1-2

_____

_____

John 14:6

_____

_____

Acts 17:24

_____

_____

Hebrews 8:13

_____

_____

Hebrews 9:1-9

_____

_____

Hebrews 19:19-20

_____

_____

Day 5: Read Matthew 27:54-66

Verses 54-61

1. (E) In contrast to the three scoffers, list the three admirers in verses 54, 55, and 57.

_____

_____

_____

_____

_____

2. (E) Matthew tells us in verses 55–56 who remained with Jesus. Who in contrast is *not* present (Matthew 26:56)?

    _____

    _____

    _____

3. (I) What stands out to you about the actions of Joseph of Arimathea?

    _____

    _____

    _____

4. (I) Why would Matthew feel it was necessary to include Jesus's burial?

    _____

    _____

    _____

5. (I) How is verse 60 a fulfillment of Isaiah 53:9?

    _____

    _____

    _____

6. (I) Read verse 61 in the Christian Standard Bible (CSB) version. How do these witnesses and their actions help alleviate any doubt you might have?

    _____

    _____

    _____

    _____

7. (I) Remember that women did not have an impact on society in Jesus's time, and their testimony was not legally binding. But here they are bearing witness to one of the greatest events in history. In what ways do these women provide a tangible expression to the teachings of Christ?

_____

_____

_____

Verses 62-66

8. (I) What did the chief priests and Pharisees seem to remember (that the disciples seemed to forget) and then inquire of Pilate?

_____

_____

_____

9. (E,I) What repeated word is found in verses 64–66? What does the author want us to keep in mind? How does God use the enemies' plans and precautions for His own glory and purpose?

_____

_____

_____

10. (T) All seems hopeless at the end of this chapter as Jesus's dead body is laid in a guarded tomb. But we know the story is not over. What circumstance in your life appears hopeless as you wait for the fulfillment of God's promise of a conquering ending?

_____

_____

_____

_____

Day 6: Commit what you learned to prayer. Reread Matthew 27.

Adoration:

"God, you are…."

Pray the attributes of God we studied this week back to God.

Confession:

"Lord, I confess…."

In light of the above and what we studied this week, what did you learn about yourself?

Thanksgiving:

"Thank you…."

What from this week's passage made your heart overflow with thanksgiving?

Supplication:

"I lift up…."

After reading this week's passage, what petitions do you need to ask of God?

Global: _____

Local: _____

Personal: _____

MATTHEW 28

We Live Because Jesus Lives

AIM: We live because Jesus lives.

Scripture to Memorize:

And behold, I am with you always, to the end of the age.

–Matt. 28:20

Attribute of God: Holy

God is set apart and distinct from His creation. The holiness of God is the sum of all His attributes. He is perfect, pure, and without sin. There is none like Him. God's holiness exposes the depth of our sin and our need for a Savior. Were it not for Jesus Christ, no sinner could stand in the presence of God's holiness. God's holiness is the only attribute in Scripture communicated in the superlative degree because it consumes the very essence of who He is.

Doctrine: Resurrection

Resurrection is the concept of coming back to life after death. If there is no Resurrection of Christ, our faith is futile, and we are still dead in our sins. His resurrection absolutely matters to believers because it validates His sacrificial death. It demonstrates the truth of His claims about Himself. There are many details presented in Scripture for the evidence of His death. It was the Roman guards who secured the tomb, His friends who prepared His body for burial and sat facing the tomb watching for any signs of life, and then of course, the empty tomb! But Praise God death could not hold Him. He truly is the Son of God. Death had no claim on Him and Satan was defeated. In death, the atonement was made. He was punished for our sin, but once the price was paid, death lost its power and after three days, Jesus was raised from the dead. Jesus experienced a full bodily resurrection. He was able to eat food, speak to the people, and friends were able to touch Him. Over 500 people saw Him alive. Resurrection is victory. One day we will also participate in this victory. This is the believer's glorious hope. There is no eternal life apart from Jesus's resurrection. We too will be resurrected. When we die, we immediately enter into the presence of the Lord, but the final resurrection has not yet happened. This is why Jesus is referred to as the fruitfruits. He led the way in life after death. While there are other resurrections mentioned in Scripture, there is one key element to Jesus's. Those others died again. But Jesus was raised to life, never to die again. One day our physical bodies will be raised from death, transformed, and glorified. We live because He lives. Jesus IS life.

Day 1: Read Matthew 28

1. In two to three sentences, summarize what happens in this chapter.

   Chapter 28

   _____

   _____

   _____

   _____

2. Matthew 28 mentions the seventh and final mountain found throughout the Gospel of Matthew. Seven represents completion. Find and list the other mentions of mountains, what events happened at those mountains, and their spiritual significance. One has been done for you.

   Matthew 4:8 – Satan tempts Jesus on a mountain

   Satan tempts Jesus to skip the cross and go straight to the crown, but in God's Kingdom, there is no glory without the suffering. His Kingdom is characterized by humility.

   _____

   _____

   _____

   _____

   _____

3. Look up the following verses and note the importance of Jesus's bodily resurrection.

    John 10:17-18

    _____

    _____

    Acts 2:31, Psalm 16:10

    _____

    _____

    Acts 17:30-31

    _____

    _____

    Romans 6:4

    _____

    _____

    Ephesians 1:18-23

    _____

    _____

    1 Thessalonians 4:13-14

    _____

    _____

    1 Peter 1:3-6

    _____

    _____

Day 2: Read Matthew 28:1-10

Verses 1-10

1. (E,I) Count how many "sees/beholds" are in verses 1-10. What do you think is the author's intent by reusing these words?

_____

_____

_____

2. (E) Fill in the blanks from verse 1.

"Now after the Sabbath, toward the _____, Mary Magdalene and the other Mary went to _____ the tomb."

3. (E,I) Who were the first to witness the resurrection? Why is that so significant?

_____

_____

_____

4. (E) What caused a great earthquake? What did the angel do?

_____

_____

_____

5. (I) Why do you think the angel rolled back the stone?

_____

_____

_____

_____

6. (E) Describe the angel's appearance and the guards' reaction. (Don't miss the irony that at Jesus's empty tomb, the guards were the ones who became like dead men.)

_____

_____

_____

_____

7. (E) Fill in the blanks of what the angel said to the women.

"Do _____ , for I know that you _____ who was crucified."

8. (I) What is the difference between the guards' fear and the women's fear?

_____

_____

_____

_____

9. (I) How is verse 6 a fulfillment of 12:38–42, 16:21, 17:23, 20:19, and 26:61?

_____

_____

_____

_____

10. (E) What were the angel's instructions to the women (vv. 6–7)?

_____

_____

_____

_____

11. (I) Why is it so important that the women "tell" someone (Romans 10:14, 17)?

_____

_____

_____

12. (I) Match the following phrases from verse 7 with the correct tense.

He has risen from the dead   Present

He is going before you to Galilee   Past

You will see Him   Future

13. (T) How are these past, present, and future principles still for us today?

_____

_____

_____

14. (E,I) How did the women respond to the angel's instructions? How did they depart—with what and with great what? How can these two emotions go hand in hand?

_____

_____

_____

_____

15. (T) Describe a time in your life when you were in a fearful situation but were still able to have great joy knowing Jesus was with you?

_____

_____

_____

_____

16. (T) Jesus's greeting to the women in verse 9 is equivalent to the modern-day *hi*. How does the fact that Jesus just appeared supernaturally yet interacted in an ordinary, everyday way impact you?

_____

_____

_____

_____

17. (E) What did the women do in verse 9 after Jesus spoke His greeting? (Read Deuteronomy 6:13.)

_____

_____

_____

_____

18. (I) What does the author want to communicate about the nature of the resurrection when he mentions the women took hold of Jesus's feet?

_____

_____

_____

_____

19. (E,I) How does Jesus refer to His disciples in verse 10? How might this term be an encouragement to the disciples (Matthew 26:56)?

_____

_____

_____

_____

20. (T) What are you prone to fear in this world? How does knowing that Christ has risen give His people hope that overcomes every reason to fear?

_____

_____

_____

Day 3: Read Matthew 28:11-15

Verses 11-15

1. (E) Summarize what happens in these verses.

_____

_____

_____

_____

2. (I) How did the guards' sharing of the news of Jesus's resurrection differ from the women's sharing?

_____

_____

_____

_____

3. (E) How did the Jewish leaders respond to the facts about Jesus's resurrection? How did the Jewish people respond?

_____

_____

_____

_____

4. (E,I) Read Matthew 27:64. What is so ironic about the story the soldiers were instructed to tell the people (vv. 11–15)?

_____

_____

_____

5. (E,I) What is the result of the soldier's lie in verse 15? How is this a fulfillment of Jesus's words in Matthew 12:38–42?

_____

_____

_____

6. (T) What other false explanations of the resurrection are prevalent in our culture today?

_____

_____

_____

7. (T) What lessons can you learn from the opposition Jesus faced from His enemies?

_____

_____

_____

8. (T) When have you personally dismissed a truth about God? What was the result?

_____

_____

_____

_____

Day 4: Read Matthew 28:16-20

Verses 16-20

1. (E) Fill in the blanks from verse 16.

   "Now the _____ disciples went to _____, to the _____ to which Jesus had directed them."

2. (I) All three words you used to fill in the blanks are significant. Give your best answer to why for each one.

   _____

   _____

   _____

3. (E,I) What were the two reactions of the disciples in verse 17 when they saw Jesus?

   _____

   _____

   _____

4. (T) How is verse 17 a picture of us all? How can we live in a place of worship and doubt?

   _____

   _____

   _____

5. (E,I,T) What important claim does Jesus make in verse 18? How have we seen this theme throughout the Gospel of Matthew? How is this both a warning and an encouragement for the disciples then and disciples now?

   _____

   _____

   _____

6. (E) In verses 19–20, Jesus states what is referred to as the "Great Commission." What two commands does Jesus give in the first part of verse 19?

   a. _____ therefore and

   b. _____.

7. (E) What two procedures does Jesus give for making disciples?

   a. _____ them in the name of the Father, Son, and Spirit,

   b. _____ them to observe all that I [Jesus] have commanded you.

8. (I) Match the mandate on the left with its spiritual significance on the right.

Baptizing them in the name of the Father, Son, and Spirit	Bring order out of chaos with God's law; ruling, subduing, and taking dominion in the very hearts of all believers.
Teaching them to observe all that I have commanded	Fill the earth with image bearers who take on the very character of God.

9. (I,T) Read the two commands God gave Adam and Even in Genesis 1:28. How do the physical terms in the creation mandate paint a spiritual truth for the commission mandate? How does this help point us to our new creation story in Jesus Christ?

   _____

   _____

   _____

10. (T) Jesus taught them to observe *all* He has commanded. Think back over the entirety of the Gospel of Matthew. What are some of Jesus's teachings that are rarely taught in churches today?

    _____

    _____

    _____

    _____

11. (T) Are you personally equipped to teach *all* that Jesus commanded? Why or why not?

_____

_____

_____

12. (E) Fill in the blank from verse 20. (Review Exodus 3:14)

"And behold, _____ with you always, to the end of the age."

13. (E) What promise does Jesus make in verse 20? Read the verses below. What do you notice? How is this a fitting end to the book of Matthew? What conclusions does Matthew leave with us?

Genesis 28:15

_____

_____

Deuteronomy 31:6-8

_____

_____

Joshua 1:5

_____

_____

1 Chronicles 28:20

_____

_____

Isaiah 41:10-13

_____

_____

Matthew 1:21-23

_____

_____

14. (I,T) Why would this truth encourage the disciples at this time? How does this truth encourage you personally?

_____

_____

_____

15. (T) What does the Great Commission look like in your life today? How do you participate in nurturing and guiding others in their faith?

_____

_____

_____

Day 5: Reread Matthew 28

1. (T) Why should we believe that Jesus came back to life from the dead?

_____

_____

_____

2. (T) If Jesus has a body, why can we not see Him?

_____

_____

_____

_____

3. (I) Explain how Jesus's last words on the cross to the Father (27:46) and Jesus's last words to the disciples (28:20) convey the very essence and message of the Gospel

_____

_____

_____

_____

Day 6: Commit what you learned to prayer. Reread Matthew 28.

Adoration:

"God, you are…."

Pray the attributes of God we studied this week back to God.

Confession:

"Lord, I confess…."

In light of the above and what we studied this week, what did you learn about yourself?

Thanksgiving:

"Thank you…."

What from this week's passage made your heart overflow with thanksgiving?

Supplication:

"I lift up…."

After reading this week's passage, what petitions do you need to ask of God?

Global: _____

Local: _____

Personal: _____

WRAP-UP

The words of the Bible are the very words of God our Creator speaking to us. They are completely truthful, they are pure, they are powerful, and they are wise and righteous. We should read these words with reverence and awe, and with joy and delight. Through these words God gives us eternal life, and daily nourishes our spiritual lives.

–ESV Scripture Journals

All Scripture is breathed out by God and profitable for teaching, for reproof, for correction, and for training in righteousness, that the man of God may be complete, equipped for every good work.

–2 Tim. 3:16-17

Day 1

1. How has the Holy Spirit used Matthew to convict you of sin? What has He revealed to you that you need to confess?

   _____

   _____

   _____

2. How has the Holy Spirit used Matthew to train you in righteousness? What in your life has God entrusted you to do? What lessons from this study of Matthew can help you grow to be spiritually strong and complete?

   _____

   _____

   _____

Day 2

1. What verse or passage from Matthew resonates with you the strongest? Why? How has the study of Matthew helped your understanding of Scripture?

_____

_____

_____

2. What aim, principle, or doctrine from Matthew stands out to you the most? Why?

_____

_____

_____

_____

3. What attribute of God stands out most after your study of Matthew? How has this insight affected your worship and prayer life?

_____

_____

_____

_____

Day 3

1. What truths about God changed your view of self?

_____

_____

_____

_____

2. How will this change the way you live?

_____

_____

_____

_____

Day 4

1. Which of the characters from Matthew have you been able to relate to the most? Explain.

_____

_____

_____

_____

2. Which of the characters from Matthew have you been able to relate to the least? Explain.

_____

_____

_____

_____

Day 5

1. How has your relationship with Jesus Christ changed during this study? What impact has that had on your relationships with others?

_____

_____

_____

Day 6: Commit what you learned to prayer

Adoration:

"God, you are…."

Pray an attribute that you learned this week about God.

Confess:

"I confess…."

In light of the above attribute, what did you learn about yourself?

Thanksgiving:

"Thank you, Father…."

What from this week's passage made your heart overflow with thanksgiving?

Supplication:

After reading this week's passage, what petition do you need to ask of God?

Global: _____

Local: _____

Personal: _____

ATTRIBUTES OF GOD

Accessible: God is near to His people. He hears and responds to His children.

Compassionate: God cares for and acts on behalf of His children.

Creator: God made everything. God alone can bring something out of nothing.

Deliverer: God rescues and saves His children.

Eternal: God exists outside of time. He always was and always will be. He is the beginning and the end.

Father: God adopts us into His family and makes us His children.

Faithful: God always keeps His promises.

Glory: The sum of all His attributes. Jesus Christ reveals God's glory completely.

Good: God will always do what is best. He promises to work all things together for good.

Gracious: God gives us what we do not deserve.

Guide: God leads us in the way we should go.

Holy: God is perfect and without sin. He is set apart from His creation.

Immutable: God never changes in His essence, character, purpose, and promises. He is the same yesterday, today, and tomorrow.

Impartial: God does not save based on merit. He saves regardless of what they have done or will do.

Incomprehensible: God is beyond our understanding. He knows all things and we can only know what He has revealed to us.

Infinite: God has no limits. He cannot be measured.

Invisible: We cannot see God or feel Him physically. He has made Himself visible through the Person of Jesus Christ.

Jealous: God will not share His glory. It rightfully belongs to Him and Him alone.

Just: God is always perfectly fair and right in all His actions.

Love: God is love. He gives Himself to Himself and to others. It is His affection for Himself and His people. He displayed His love by sending His Son, Jesus Christ as the Savior of the world.

Merciful: God does not give His children the punishment they deserve.

Omnipotent: God is all powerful. He has unlimited power and authority. What He wills, He accomplishes.

Omnipresent: God is fully present everywhere. He exists outside of time and space.

Omniscient: God knows everything past, present, and future. He is never surprised. Nothing is hidden from Him.

Patient: God is slow to anger. He endures humanity's flaws to give time for repentance.

Perfect: Completely free from sin, defect, or fault. Everything He does is right. This is how and why Scripture is without error.

Person: God has an identity and personality. He is one being in three persons with a mind and a will and is able to communicate.

Preserver: God always finishes what He starts. He will continue to do the good work He started in us.

Provider: God meets the needs of His children.

Refuge: God is a place of safety and protection.

Righteous: God is always right in all He does.

Savior: God rescues sinners from the penalty of death and hell. Jesus lived a perfect life and fulfilled justice in His death.

Self-Existent: God depends on nothing and no one for life or existence.

Self-Sufficient: God has no need for anything.

Sovereign: God controls all things.

Transcendent: God is far above humans in being and actions.

Truth: What God says is reality and can be relied upon.

Wrath: God hates sin and all unrighteousness.

Wise: God knows what is best and acts accordingly. All wisdom comes from God.

Worthy: God deserves all glory, honor, and praise.

SPECIAL THANKS

I would like to thank B Joye Watson from Dumas, Texas for designing the cover art and Lorie Shafer of Dumas, Texas for the author picture. I would like to give a special thanks to all the women who have allowed me to share my love of teaching the Bible with them.

WHAT IS THE GOSPEL?

The Gospel means good news. This is the Good News of Jesus Christ and the way to salvation. The bad news is we are all sinners. The wages of sin is death and hell for all eternity. We have broken God's laws and in order for us to dwell with God, sin must be removed or paid for. The Old Testament established that sin can only be removed by the shedding of blood. God rich in mercy, grace, love, and justice sent His Son Jesus to die on the cross. His death was the sin offering that fulfilled all the Old Testament law required. He lived a perfect life and was sinless in thought, word and action. We cannot do anything to save ourselves. We cannot earn our salvation. The only way to salvation is placing our faith in the life, death, and resurrection of Christ. For those who are in Christ Jesus, there is no condemnation. He has taken the punishment we deserved – death- defeated death in His resurrection and in exchange has given us His righteousness. We are counted perfect so when God looks at us He sees the righteousness of His Son. Through Jesus Christ, we are able to dwell and live in God's presence. We will not spend eternity in hell, but in God's presence. This is all a gift of God. It is by His grace, through faith in Christ Jesus we have been saved. (Ephesians 2:8-9)